IN SOVEREIGN HANDS

JIM DYET, LARRY GREEN, ALEX BAUMAN

IN SOVEREIGN HANDS

EZRA AND ESTHER

This inductive Bible study is designed for individual, small group, or classroom use. A leader's guide with full lesson plans and the answers to the Bible study questions is available from Regular Baptist Press. Order RBP1695 online at www.regularbaptistpress.org, e-mail orders@rbpstore.org, call toll-free 1-800-727-4440, or contact your distributor.

REGULAR BAPTIST PRESS
1300 North Meacham Road
Schaumburg, Illinois 60173-4806

The King James Version is the English translation used in our Sunday School curriculum.

The Doctrinal Basis of Our Curriculum

A more detailed statement with references is available upon request.

- The verbal, plenary inspiration of the Scriptures
- Only one true God
- The Trinity of the Godhead
- The Holy Spirit and His ministry
- The personality of Satan
- The Genesis account of creation
- Original sin and the fall of man
- The virgin birth of Christ
- Salvation through faith in the shed blood of Christ
- The bodily resurrection and priesthood of Christ
- Grace and the new birth
- Justification by faith
- Sanctification of the believer

- The security of the believer
- The church
- The ordinances of the local church: baptism by immersion and the Lord's Supper
- Biblical separation— ecclesiastical and personal
- Obedience to civil government
- The place of Israel
- The pretribulation rapture of the church
- The premillennial return of Christ
- The millennial reign of Christ
- Eternal glory in Heaven for the righteous
- Eternal torment in Hell for the wicked

IN SOVEREIGN HANDS: EZRA AND ESTHER
Adult Bible Study Book
Vol. 55, No. 5
© 2007
Regular Baptist Press • Schaumburg, Illinois
www.regularbaptistpress.org • 1-800-727-4440
Printed in U.S.A.
All rights reserved
RBP1698 • ISBN: 978-1-59402-460-3

Contents

Preface

Have you ever asked yourself, "Where is God?" When everything around you seems unsettled and uncertain, have you agonized over the purposes and plan of God? Maybe you have doubted His providential care or failed to discern His comforting presence. If you have, then rest assured that exposure to the books of Ezra and Esther will encourage your heart, instruct your mind, and help you develop strong, courageous faith. You will learn, as the Jews learned, that God is there even when you think He isn't. He hasn't forgotten you. He does care, and He is in control.

God is faithful to His promises, providentially protecting and providing for His people while accomplishing His plan. How we need to be reminded of this great truth. Though He is invisible, God is invincible. The book of Ezra demonstrates the timeless truth that God keeps His promises. He promised to release His people from the Babylonian captivity, and He did so—right on schedule! Through the drama and suspense of the book of Esther, we see God's omnipotence and tender care. God turned apparent tragedy into amazing triumph as He intervened in the political affairs of Persia to deliver His people.

As we study these two Old Testament books, we will discover a variety of means God used to accomplish His purposes. Consider a few of the people and events He employed: decrees of pagan rulers, the prepared heart of a scribe, the anger of a Persian king, the assassination plot of a few conspirators, and the arrogance of a pagan prince. These elements remind us that God cares for His people. He does not abandon them.

May your study of Ezra and Esther help you perceive God at work in your world and life. May it prompt you to praise Him for His continual care and protective presence, and may it persuade you to place your trust and confidence in Him as He works out His purposes for His glory and your good.

Trusting God's Promises

God keeps His promises.

Ezra 1; 2

"According as his divine power hath given unto us all things that pertain unto life and godliness, through the knowledge of him that hath called us to glory and virtue: Whereby are given unto us exceeding great and precious promises: that by these ye might be partakers of the divine nature, having escaped the corruption that is in the world through lust" (2 Peter 1:3, 4).

Imagine you are lying in a hospital bed and are being prepped for open-heart surgery when a nurse comes in and says, "I'm sorry, we'll have to reschedule your surgery for tomorrow. The doctor didn't show up today as he had promised he would." Most likely your next words would be something like, "Get me out of here!" When our lives are at stake, we want someone who is faithful and trustworthy.

No one has been making promises longer than God has. From eternity past, God has been faithful to His word. His history is spotless and unmatched. He is completely trustworthy. This study steps into a low point in Israel's history, recorded in the book of Ezra, and finds God's people in captivity nine hundred miles from Jerusalem. But their days

got brighter, for their sovereign God was on the move and was about
to show Himself faithful once again. His people would go home to the
Promised Land for the first time in seventy years.

Getting Started

1. Describe someone you know who faithfully keeps his or her
promises.

2. What if God were only as reliable as the person you described?
How would that change your life?

Searching the Scriptures

God's Promises of Judgment

God keeps His promises. Some of those promises, like the one He
made to the Israelites in Joshua 24:20, serve as warnings.

3. Read Joshua 24:20. What did God promise the Israelites through
Joshua?

4. Read 2 Chronicles 36:15 and 16. How did the Israelites respond
to the warnings that God graciously sent them?

In 588 BC, seventy-two years before the opening events of the book
of Ezra, Nebuchadnezzar, king of Babylon, laid siege to Jerusalem for
a year and a half. His siege was directed by God in fulfillment of His
promise to discipline the Israelites if they turned their backs on Him.

The siege ended when Nebuchadnezzar captured Zedekiah, king of Judah, and took him to Riblah. There Nebuchadnezzar killed Zedekiah's sons and then gouged out Zedekiah's eyes. After one final raid of the temple in Jerusalem in 586 BC, Nebuchadnezzar torched it and dragged Zedekiah and those who still remained in Judah to exile in Babylon (2 Kings 25:8–21; Jeremiah 39:1–9).

During their seventy years of captivity, devout Jews longed to return to their homeland and to Jerusalem, its capital. They would never feel at home in Babylon!

5. Read Psalm 137:1–6. Describe the mood of the Jews in Babylon.

6. What did they ask God to do to them if they forgot Jerusalem (v. 6)?

7. If you had to spend decades or the rest of your life in a country opposed to the culture and worship you had enjoyed in your homeland, how would you feel?

God's Promises of Restoration

8. Read Jeremiah 32:37–44. What promises did God give to Israel through Jeremiah?

God never left His people without hope (Jeremiah 31:17). Even before the people of Judah were led captive, God promised that He would restore them to the Promised Land. No doubt the captives clung to God's promises of future grace and mercy.

9. What promise or promises are you waiting for the Lord to fulfill?

10. Read Titus 1:2. How can you be sure the Lord will keep His word?

Eventually the cloud of despair over the captive Jews lifted, because God worked in the heart of Cyrus, king of Persia, to make the return of the Jews possible. The hand of the King of the universe can move the heart of any earthly king. Cyrus ruled a vast empire after crushing the mighty Babylonians in 539 BC and wresting their power from them. In 538 BC, the first year of his reign over that extensive empire, Cyrus issued a decree permitting Jewish captives to leave Babylon and return to Judah (Ezra 1:1–3). This action was in keeping with his humanitarian policy of restoring displaced people to their homelands.

About two hundred years before Cyrus was born, God had identified him by name as the initiator of this return. Through the prophet Isaiah, God had announced that Cyrus "is my shepherd, and shall perform all my pleasure: even saying to Jerusalem, Thou shalt be built; and to the temple, Thy foundation shall be laid" (Isaiah 44:28).

God's Power to Keep Promises

It is encouraging to know that God "stirred up the spirit of Cyrus" to decree the Jews' return home (Ezra 1:1). Without God's working, Cyrus would never have made such a decree.

11. Read Proverbs 21:1. How does this verse portray the power of God?

God's power unleashed to fulfill His promises concerning the return from Captivity has not diminished; God is still "able to do exceeding abundantly above all that we ask or think" (Ephesians 3:20).

12. How might a Christian strengthen his or her confidence in God's power?

Cyrus seems to have been well informed about his place in God's plan to restore the Jews to the Promised Land. Perhaps the prophet Daniel, who was still living in Babylon when Cyrus decreed the return of the Jews, had notified Cyrus about God's prophecies concerning him.

13. Read Ezra 1:2 and 3. What conclusions had Cyrus drawn about God?

Just as the Lord had "stirred up the spirit of Cyrus" (v. 1) to allow the Jews to return home, so He stirred the spirits of many Jews to seize the opportunity to participate in the expedition (v. 5). Family chiefs from the tribes of Judah and Benjamin, priests and Levites, and many others decided to journey to Jerusalem because God had touched their hearts. The thought of going to Jerusalem was attractive, but the desire to stay in Babylon was also strong. Many of those who could make the trip to Jerusalem were born in Babylon and had heard only of Jerusalem. Leaving their established homes and families for a burned-out city nine hundred miles away was a hard choice to make. But God's power through His Spirit made them willing and eager to go.

God's Provision for His Promises

Those who chose not to return to Jerusalem because of old age, as in Daniel's case, or for some other reason, contributed generously to the expedition. Also, Cyrus required those who weren't even Jews to give something toward the Jews' expedition (v. 6).

14. Read Ezra 1:6. What did the returnees get from their neighbors?

15. With what attitude did they give away their goods?

Freely giving away goods without any perceivable benefit to the giver is unnatural. God's hand was at work once again in moving the hearts of the people to give and thereby supply what the returnees would need to survive the four-month trip and the first few months in Israel. Also, the unity provided clear evidence that God was working in the lives of His people.

Cyrus not only decreed the expedition but also contributed to its success. He restored the vessels Nebuchadnezzar had stolen from the temple of the Lord and placed in his heathen temple (v. 7). Mithredath, Cyrus's treasurer, counted these articles and handed them over to Sheshbazzar, the prince of Judah (v. 8). The tally was 30 gold dishes, 1,000 silver dishes, 29 knives, 30 gold bowls, 410 silver bowls of another kind, and 1,000 other articles (vv. 9, 10). These articles plus others not included in the above list totaled 5,400 (v. 11).

The Recipients of God's Promises

Zerubbabel led the first return from Babylon (2:1, 2). Ezra was not among the first wave of returnees to Jerusalem; he arrived later, in 457 BC. Some Bible teachers believe Sheshbazzar (1:11) and Zerubbabel (2:2) were the same person. Others believe Sheshbazzar was Zerubbabel's uncle and that he died before the foundation of the temple was completed. Interestingly, Zerubbabel's name appears in the messianic lineage of Jesus (Matthew 1:12).

Ezra categorized the returnees as Zerubbabel and other leaders (v. 2), the families (vv. 3–35), the priests (vv. 36–39), Levites, (vv. 40–42), Nethinim (temple workers, vv. 43–54), descendants of Solomon's servants (vv. 55–58), and families without proof of their genealogy (vv. 59–62). Priests with an uncertain genealogy would not be allowed to serve as priests until a high priest could use the Urim and Thummim to ascertain their genealogy (v. 63). The Urim and Thummim were stones on the high priest's breastplate that God used to convey His will.

In all, 42,360 Jews and their 7,337 servants made the trip. Two hundred singers among those servants were employed to sing (v. 65).

16. Do you think the singers sang as the returnees traveled to Jerusalem? If so, what do you think they sang about?

17. What do you think characterized the moods of their songs?

Animals went along too: 736 horses, 245 mules, 435 camels, and 6,720 donkeys (vv. 64–67). They served as ancient U-Hauls for the returnees' adventure in moving. Quite an entourage trekked nine hundred miles to Jerusalem! The journey must have required faith and dedication on the part of those who made the long trip home.

Consider what it must have been like to be on the road for nearly four months, traveling about nine hundred miles to Jerusalem and then finding the temple in ruins. Surely the sight must have brought tears to the returnees' eyes. However, undaunted by what they saw and inspired by what they hoped to see—a rebuilt temple—the returnees prepared for the work that awaited them. Some heads of families gave generously to the building fund "after their ability" (Ezra 2:68, 69). Their offering equaled about 1,100 pounds of gold and three tons of silver as well as 100 priestly garments.

18. What kind of an offering would you expect from the returnees shortly after they arrived in Israel to find no place to live?

19. What did the Jews demonstrate by their generous giving (Ezra 2:68, 69)?

All was in place for the work to begin. "All Israel" was home at last (v. 70).

Exiled Israel became the focal point of God's sovereign actions. He moved the heart of Cyrus, a pagan king, to decree the Jews' return home, and He moved the hearts of many Jews to participate in that return. Everything that occurred to move thousands of displaced Jews from Babylon to the Promised Land was orchestrated in fulfillment of what God had promised. He always keeps His word.

Making It Personal

20. How has knowing that God is faithful to His promises affected your life?

21. Read John 14 this week. Which promises relate to

    a. your future?

    b. your prayers?

    c. your well-being?

22. Which of God's promises, in John 14 or elsewhere, do you find most difficult to claim?

23. What action will you take this week to demonstrate your renewed belief that God keeps His word?

24. Memorize 2 Peter 1:3 and 4.

Following God, Finding Joy

God gives joy to those who follow Him.

Ezra 3

"And they sang together by course in praising and giving thanks unto the LORD; because he is good, for his mercy endureth for ever toward Israel. And all the people shouted with a great shout, when they praised the LORD, because the foundation of the house of the LORD was laid" (Ezra 3:11).

Johann M. Haydn, who wrote the music for a number of lively hymns, including "O Worship the King," was asked why his music was so cheerful. He responded, "I cannot make it otherwise. I write according to the thoughts I feel; when I think upon my God, my heart is so full of joy that the notes dance and leap from my pen; and since God has given me a cheerful heart, it will be pardoned me that I serve him with a cheerful spirit."

Where does such a cheerful spirit come from? Is there a secret formula? Is there a special program that guarantees a cheerful heart? This lesson will address these questions by looking at Jews who learned what it takes to have a joyful heart.

Getting Started

1. What does the world believe brings joy?

2. What have you tried to do to bring joy to your life?

Searching the Scriptures

Glorifying God

3. Read Ezra 3:1. What ideas does the phrase "as one man" bring to your mind?

The people of Israel "gathered themselves together as one man" (Ezra 3:1). This statement describes the Jews' unity of purpose. They were all devoted to seeing the temple rebuilt. But the rebuilding was more of a secondary purpose. Their primary purpose was to see God glorified, for they were His Chosen People. But the ash heap that Jerusalem had become was embarrassing to the Jews and was a poor testimony of God before the nations around Israel.

4. Why doesn't purposing to be happy in life lead to happiness?

The assembled Jews wanted to worship God, but they had no temple. They didn't even have an altar. But they had a mandate from God to rebuild the temple. So they began by erecting an altar where the former altar had stood (vv. 2, 3).

Fearing God

Erecting the altar sent a message to the nations around Israel: the Jews were serious about resettling the land, reestablishing their worship, and reconstructing Jerusalem. As the altar went up, so did the danger the Jews faced from surrounding nations. This threat caused the Jews to fear (v. 3).

5. Read Ezra 3:3. Whom did the Jews fear more, their enemies or God? How can you tell?

6. Read Psalm 27. How does this psalm of David reflect the sentiments of the remnant as they erected the altar?

The Jews must have believed—and rightly so—that acting on their fear of God rather than on their fear of other people was the better choice. If happiness had been their purpose for living, then they would not have erected the altar in order to avoid conflict. But they chose instead to stick to their purpose to glorify God.

After all, the ash heap around them served as a constant reminder that God wants His people to fear Him and that He loves them enough to discipline them until they do. True happiness never comes through fearing people more than God.

Obeying God's Word

7. Read Ezra 3:2. How carefully did the leaders treat the Word of God?

God had decreed through Moses that Israel was required to assemble annually for the Feast of Trumpets, the Day of Atonement, and the Feast of Tabernacles (Leviticus 23:23–44). The seventh month in the Jewish calendar (part of our September and October) was the designated month for these three feasts. The Jews took God's Word seriously. They didn't hold a forum to decide whether to obey it or to make up their own rules. Nor did they make up an excuse for not obeying God's Word right away. The purpose of the returning Jews was to glorify God. This purpose led them to fear God, which in turn led them to obey God.

8. What excuses might the Jews have used to forgo celebrating the feasts during their first year back in the land?

9. When, if ever, have you found lasting satisfaction in disobeying God? Describe a time when your heart was refreshed because you diligently obeyed God.

The Jews' obedience to God's Word was invigorating. It led them to worship Him together.

10. Read Ezra 3:2–6. How many times is a form of the word "offer" used in these verses?

11. What does the frequency of this word tell you about the Jews' mind-set?

Significantly, God gave both Jeshua and Zerubbabel to Israel as leaders (v. 8). These two men shared the challenge of rebuilding the temple and preparing the people for life and worship in Judah. Jeshua, a descendant of Aaron the high priest, directed the nation's religious life, and Zerubbabel, a descendant of King David, directed its civil life.

Before laying the foundation for the temple, the returnees worshiped the Lord with burnt offerings morning and evening (v. 3). They also observed the Feast of Tabernacles (v. 4). This weeklong feast, kept from the 15th to the 22nd day of the seventh month, commemorated Israel's living in tents during the people's long sojourn in the wilderness between Egypt and Canaan. Throughout this festival the worshipers lived in booths, or huts, constructed of leafy branches, and they offered daily sacrifices as prescribed by the law of Moses (Leviticus 23:34–43).

Throughout Israel's history the Feast of Tabernacles marked the harvest of the land (Leviticus 23:39). It was also the occasion when Solomon dedicated the temple he had built for the Lord (2 Chronicles 5:3). Appropriately, the first wave of returnees from Babylon kept the Feast of Tabernacles, for they themselves were the first harvest gathered into Judah from the Captivity. Their participation in the festival pictured a future time when God will save Jews from every tribe, pluck them out of every region of the world, and gather them to Israel. When that time occurs, redeemed Israel will celebrate the Feast of Tabernacles in the presence of her Messiah.

After observing the Feast of Tabernacles, the Jews from Babylon presented burnt offerings for the new moons, sacrifices for all the feasts of the Lord, and freewill offerings too (Ezra 3:5). They had been offering burnt offerings from the first day of the seventh month, when they had first gathered in Jerusalem, but they had not begun to lay the foundation for the temple (v. 6).

12. What must be true of a person's worship of God if it's never followed by service to God?

Getting to Work

The time to assemble construction materials for the temple had come. By the authority of Cyrus's decree and drawing from the resources they had accumulated in Babylon, the Jews paid the construction workers and purchased cedar from Lebanon (v. 7). Solomon had used cedar from Lebanon in his temple (2 Chronicles 2:8, 9). The timber from Lebanon would be loaded onto rafts, shipped along the Mediterranean coastal waters, unloaded at Joppa, and hauled to the construction site in Jerusalem (Ezra 3:7). The temple workers' spirits must have soared when the first shipment of cedar logs arrived.

In the second month of the second year of their repatriation, the Jews began to build. This was about nine months after they had kept the Feast of Tabernacles. Zerubbabel gave some Levites from three family groups the responsibility to supervise the construction of the temple (vv. 8, 9). The supervisors included young and old alike.

13. Read Ezra 3:9. The overseers of the construction "stood . . . together," or "arose as one," to do the work of the Lord. To what do you attribute their unity?

14. No doubt laying the foundation of the temple was hard work. How do you think the hard work affected the spirits of those who put in long days of service for the Lord?

At last, in 535 BC, the temple workers finished laying the foundation. They had completed the first phase of the construction, but many challenges lay ahead. Some of those challenges would eventually delay the finishing of the temple.

Rejoicing

Every congregation that has completed a building program after faithfully praying, planning, and plodding has experienced great joy upon seeing the finished product. Although the Jews had completed only the first phase of their building project, they celebrated joyfully and loudly. The priests clothed in priestly garments blew trumpets, and the Levites who were descendants of Asaph played cymbals (Ezra 3:10). Their music bounded skyward as praise to the Lord.

Songs of praise and thanksgiving also ascended from the musicians. They sang in antiphonal chorus (responsive singing between two groups) as they praised the Lord for His loving-kindness and goodness toward Israel. Recognizing that the foundation of the temple stood as evidence of the Lord's goodness and loving-kindness, the people responded to the priests and Levites' acclamations. "And all the people shouted with a great shout, when they praised the LORD, because the foundation of the house of the LORD was laid" (v. 11). Joy filled the air.

15. Read Ezra 3:11. Why did the Jews sing of God's goodness? Did they forget what had happened to them and their people? Did they not notice the strewn remnants of Solomon's glorious temple?

16. What did the Jews' united purpose to glorify God, recorded in Ezra 3:1, have to do with the experiences recorded in verse 11?

While the majority of onlookers at the temple's foundation celebrated the event joyfully, some looked on sadly. Remembering Solomon's temple, many old priests, Levites, and heads of families sobbed. Their loud wailing reached such a high decibel level that it competed with the sound of the other onlookers' joyful shouts (vv. 12, 13).

Perhaps the old men wept because they recalled the Babylonians' villainous desecration of Solomon's temple. Or they may have wept because they thought the rebuilt temple would be smaller and less glorious than Solomon's temple. Or perhaps they wept for what they had lost. Regret often leads to tears. Their past disobedience cost them years of peace and joy with the Lord in His temple. Seeing the foundation again reminded them of what could have been. Years of separation from God's temple would have caused them to grow numb to their longing for it. Seeing the foundation laid would have made those desires real again. Whatever the reason for their wailing, the elders needed to eventually move beyond it and join in the rejoicing for what God was doing in the present.

17. How does focusing on the "good ol' days" in a church's history hamper its opportunity for future good days?

God is most interested in what is happening now. There is a time for reflection on history, but dwelling on past glories or defeats won't help a church move forward and experience the joy of the Lord.

Those who heard the mingled noises of exuberance and wailing at the temple site couldn't distinguish one sound from the other. The noise was so loud that even faraway neighbors heard it (Ezra 3:13). Those neighbors would soon come calling.

Making It Personal

Most of the Jews who were in Judah when Nebuchadnezzar conquered the land were predominantly preoccupied with finding happiness in life. They had forgotten God and didn't believe His ways were worth following. They sought other gods instead.

The repatriates learned from the earlier Jews' example that joy can be found only in living for the Lord. Their own positive example challenges us to examine our lives to see if we are looking for joy outside of Jesus.

18. How joyful have you been recently? Rate yourself on the following scale.

Not at all   0   1   2   3   4   5   Extremely

19. If your life isn't characterized by joy, think through the key points from Ezra 3. Check the areas that you need to work on in your life.

❏ Resolve to glorify God (v. 1).

❏ Fear God above people (vv. 2, 3).

❏ Know and obey God's Word (vv. 2, 4–6).

❏ Serve God (vv. 7–9).

20. Write two actions you can take in one or two of these areas.

Notice that none of the areas listed under question 19 have to do with things or your situation in life. True joy comes only from being rightly related to God.

21. Memorize Ezra 3:11 as a reminder of the example of the faithfulness of God's people.

Just When Everything Was Going So Well!

God's workers can expect opposition.

Ezra 4

"Be sober, be vigilant; because your adversary the devil, as a roaring lion, walketh about, seeking whom he may devour" (1 Peter 5:8).

On December 9, 1861, Senator James W. Grimes (Iowa) introduced a bill designed to "promote the efficiency of the Navy." The bill, which was passed twelve days later, authorized the production of two hundred Medals of Honor to be "bestowed upon such petty officers, seamen, landsmen and marines as shall distinguish themselves by their gallantry in action and other seamanlike qualities during the present war [Civil War]." President Abraham Lincoln signed the bill, creating the Navy Medal of Honor.

Senator Henry Wilson (Massachusetts) introduced a similar bill to award medals "to privates in the Army of the United States who shall distinguish themselves in battle." President Lincoln signed a modified version of the bill on July 12, 1862, instituting the Army Medal of Honor.

In the years since Lincoln signed those bills into law, nearly 3,500 soldiers have received Congressional Medals of Honor. All of those soldiers have one thing in common: they gallantly faced opposition while in action for the United States. Being a soldier is like living the Christian life. When you are active, you can expect opposition. Sometimes it takes a gallant effort to overcome that opposition.

Getting Started

1. How would you respond to someone who says being active in service for the Lord isn't worth the risks?

2. Why is it important for a believer to know that the more he or she lives for God, the more Satan will target him or her?

Searching the Scriptures

The Enemy's Plan A: Deception

When the Jews finally laid the foundation of the temple, they celebrated and rejoiced with such vigor that those who were afar off heard them (Ezra 3:13). The neighboring people, already wary of what was happening at the old temple site, were even more concerned that a revival of Jerusalem was actually possible. Soon they slipped into Jerusalem with what seemed like a nice, neighborly offer.

3. Read Ezra 4:1 and 2. What were the Jews offered by their neighbors?

4. What would have been attractive about that offer? What might the Jews have gained from enlisting the help of their neighbors?

5. What might have really been motivating the Jews' neighbors?

Without hesitation the Jews turned down the Samaritans' request. Zerubbabel, Jeshua, and the other leaders told them, "Ye have nothing to do with us to build an house unto our God; but we ourselves together will build unto the LORD God of Israel" (v. 3).

These seemingly helpful neighbors were actually "adversaries" to the Jews (v. 1). They were Samaritans who grew up in the land after the Assyrians conquered the Northern Kingdom. After deporting many Israelites, the king of Assyria repopulated Israel with foreigners. In time the foreign population in Israel married Israelites who had not been deported, and their descendants became known as Samaritans. Since the Samaritans combined elements of their native, pagan religions with the worship of Jehovah, their religion was corrupt. The Jews despised the Samaritans for their intermarrying and their hybrid religion. The leaders saw through the Samaritans' facade and realized that the Samaritans were just trying to infiltrate and destroy their building efforts.

The unseen player behind the Samaritans' attempt to infiltrate the Jews was Satan. He didn't want the temple in Jerusalem to ever be rebuilt.

6. Read 2 Corinthians 11:14 and 15 and 1 Peter 5:8. What warnings about Satan do these verses include?

7. What deceptive lies does Satan tell believers?

8. What can a believer do to recognize and reject Satan's lies? (See John 17:14–17.)

The Enemy's Plan B: Discouragement

The Samaritans weren't allowed to infiltrate the Jews, so they followed Plan B—they tried to discourage the Jews. Ezra 4:4 reports, "Then the people of the land weakened the hands of the people of Judah, and troubled them in building." "Weakened the hands" is a figure of speech. The Jews' hands were "weak" because the people became discouraged and disheartened. Their passion to do the work had dissipated. The Jews didn't feel like lifting their hands to build the temple. The excitement of seeing the foundation laid was gone.

9. Read Ezra 4:4. Imagine you were one of the builders. What could your adversaries do or say to discourage you from continuing to work?

10. What might Satan use to discourage believers from being active in God's work today?

Somehow the Samaritans intimidated the builders. Perhaps they threatened them or actually carried out their threats by raiding the construction site or vandalizing the builders' homes. They even hired counselors against the builders.

11. Read Ezra 4:5. For what reason did the Samaritans hire counselors against the Jews?

Remember that building the temple wasn't the Jews' only purpose. They ultimately wanted to glorify God. Stopping the work would reflect badly on God.

Probably some of the counselors were advisers to the king. Apparently then, as now, some politicians could be bought. For about fifteen years—for the rest of Cyrus's reign, through the reign of Cambyses, and into the reign of Darius—the Samaritans kept on discouraging the Jews (v. 5).

The Devil relentlessly dogs the steps of anyone who tries to serve God. Although he carries a big bag of wrecking tools, discouragement seems to be his favorite tool. He uses it frequently to destroy initiative and to pry believers from the work God gave them to do. Discouragement usually feeds on destructive criticism or difficult circumstances. Alone or together such criticism and circumstances can sap the strength and determination of any believer who lets down his or her guard. When a believer diverts attention from God's sufficiency and focuses instead on negative words and circumstances, it isn't long until that believer quits and abandons God's work.

12. Read John 16:33. What did Jesus predict for His disciples?

13. What encouragement did He offer?

14. Read Numbers 13:25—14:4. Decades before the Hebrews possessed Canaan, they faced a historic decision. What role did discouragement play in their decision?

15. Read Numbers 14:9. On what basis did Joshua and Caleb try to encourage the Hebrews to possess Canaan?

16. What has the Lord used to encourage you when you were ready to quit?

Centuries after the events in Ezra, the disciples faced discouraging circumstances. How do you think Simon Peter, Andrew, James, and John felt after fishing all night and catching nothing? Were they discouraged? Absolutely! Were they worn out? Yes! But Jesus didn't want them to go home frustrated and fishless. So He commanded Simon to launch out into deep water and throw the nets into the sea again (Luke 5:4). Obediently, but probably with some skepticism in their hearts, Simon and his brother, Andrew, obliged Jesus; and to their astonishment, they hauled in an enormous number of fish. It took the combined effort of all four fishermen to haul the fish into their boats (vv. 5–7). The word of the Lord had led those four men from failure to success and from discouragement to the joy of discovering something remarkable about Jesus Christ: He is Lord (v. 8).

Perhaps what appears to be the right time to give up may be a good to time to start up again. This was true in the disciples' fishing experience. It may prove true for a discouraged parent who feels that his or her parenting is a hopeless task. It may be true for a discouraged Christian worker whose service for the Lord hasn't produced any tangible results. It may be true for a discouraged believer whose witness and prayers for an unsaved friend or loved one haven't borne fruit yet. For Christian workers, quitting time doesn't arrive until they have completed the tasks the Lord has assigned. The Scriptures encourage us to keep on doing the Lord's work.

17. Galatians 6:9. What promise does this verse give to diligent men and women in the Lord's work?

The result of the Samaritans' attempts to discourage the Jews is recorded in Ezra 4:24.

18. Read Ezra 4:24. What effect did the Samaritans' attempts to discourage the builders have on the project?

The Enemy's Plan C: False Accusations

Ezra 4:6–23 diverts our focus from events after the temple's foundation was laid to events in the time of Ahasuerus (Xerxes), king of Persia, fifty years later (486 BC). By this time the temple had been finished for thirty years.

The Samaritans were still causing trouble. They were hoping to thwart the restoration of Jerusalem. This time the Samaritans slandered the Jews in a letter to Ahasuerus. Though we don't know the details or specific results of this letter-writing episode, we can be sure that it hindered the Jews' progress in rebuilding Jerusalem.

Ezra 4:7–9 informs us that later, around 464 BC, Israel's enemies sent another letter to a Persian ruler—this time to Artaxerxes. It seems the Samaritans had hired two Persian officials, Rehum and Shimshai, to accuse the Jews of plotting mischief against Persia. Their goal was to stop the Jews from rebuilding the walls of Jerusalem.

Written in Aramaic, the letter carried the endorsement of several judges, governors, and officials, whom the Persian emperor must have held in high regard. The letter represented the interests of transplanted inhabitants of Samaria and Syria (vv. 10, 11). It claimed that the Jews were fortifying Jerusalem to resist taxation (vv. 12, 13). Unless Artaxerxes took swift action against the Jews, the letter reasoned, he would lose revenue and the Jews' spirit of revolution would spread to other territories in the realm (vv. 13–15). Eventually, they warned, the king would lose all his territories west of the Euphrates (v. 16).

19. Imagine you were part of the construction team in Jerusalem. What one word would you use to describe your response to the letter sent to Artaxerxes (vv. 11–16)?

The letter to Artaxerxes was deceitful and conniving. But the Jews shouldn't have expected otherwise. God's enemies, led by Satan himself, play by only one rule: do whatever it takes to win.

20. Read John 8:44. What characteristics of Satan are evident in the letter to Artaxerxes (Ezra 4:11–16)?

The king's reply, also written in Aramaic, was decisive. Artaxerxes said he had searched the archives and discovered that historically Jerusalem had been a rebellious city. Therefore, he ordered a halt to the rebuilding of Jerusalem (Ezra 4:17–22). Delighted with this response,

Rehum, Shimshai, and their associates hurried to Jerusalem and forcefully compelled the Jews to stop rebuilding the city (v. 23). Their plan
seemed to work, but God would eventually intervene. He was still in
control, and His plans could never be thwarted.

Sometimes life seems unfair. We do what is right and end up hurt or
at a loss. If we become discouraged and give up, the enemy has won.
We must continue to trust God and stay active in our service for Him.

Making It Personal

As the key verse points out, our adversary, the Devil, is on the
prowl. He stalks us, looking for a weakness in us that he can use to defeat us. For many Christians, discouragement is the biggest weakness. It
may be yours too.

21. Meditate upon the Lord's character this week. Which characteristics of the Lord encourage you to serve Him?

22. Remember to take your disappointments and discouragement to
the Lord. Bearing them alone will make you weak and will give Satan
an opportunity to defeat you. Write a prayer to the Lord, telling Him
about any discouragement you might be experiencing, and He will encourage you (1 Peter 5:7).

23. Write an encouraging note to your pastor, a missionary, or another vocational Christian worker this week. Just because that person is
in leadership doesn't mean he or she is exempt from discouragement.
In fact, the person's position makes him or her a bigger target for Satan.
The person needs to hear from you!

24. Memorize 1 Peter 5:8.

Back to Work!

God expects and enables His people
to do His will.

Ezra 5:1—6:15

"Therefore, my beloved brethren, be ye stedfast, unmoveable, always abounding in the work of the Lord, forasmuch as ye know that your labour is not in vain in the Lord" (1 Corinthians 15:58).

Winston Churchill said in a 1942 speech, presumably about World War II, "This is not the end. It is not even the beginning of the end. But it is, perhaps, the end of the beginning." The same could be said of the Jews who had laid the foundation of the new temple. Their efforts were the end of the beginning. Unfortunately many of the Jews saw their efforts as the end of the end. When God accomplishes something great in the life of a believer, it, too, is just the end of the beginning. There is always more to do in the Christian life. God expects believers to do His will, and He promises His enabling along the way.

Getting Started

1. What kind of project have you left unfinished for a long time?

2. Why haven't you finished that project?

Searching the Scriptures

The repatriated Jews became quite comfortable in Judah after their adversaries successfully stopped the construction of the temple. At that point the Jews had built only the foundation. In the ensuing fifteen years, however, they built comfortable houses for themselves. That's when God used two prophets, Haggai and Zechariah, to afflict the comfortable and to stir them up to resume work on the temple.

The Jews saw the foundation of the temple for fifteen years. Undoubtedly some of them came to believe that the temple would never be completed.

3. Imagine you were part of the construction team that laid the temple's foundation. How many years would go by before you began to believe the temple would never be finished?

Haggai and Zechariah prophesied to the Jews "in the name of the God of Israel" (Ezra 5:1). They were God's representatives with God's message for God's people. Such a combination produces the results God desires.

Paneled Homes

The repatriated Jews became a new nation with an old bad habit—they put their own interests ahead of God's. They argued that it wasn't time to build the Lord's house (Haggai 1:2); however, sixteen years earlier God had dispatched them to Jerusalem from Babylon specifically to rebuild the temple.

4. What are some excuses believers give today for not carrying out the Lord's will?

5. Read Haggai 1:2–4. What had the Israelites been building instead of constructing the temple?

6. From where did the wood for their "ceiled" (paneled) houses probably come? (See Ezra 3:7.)

The repatriated Jews weren't the first to panel their houses with cedar. Solomon lavishly paneled his house with cedar (1 Kings 7:1–3). Later God condemned King Jehoahaz for his covetous desire for a cedar-paneled home (Jeremiah 21:11–17). Perhaps the Jews were trying to regain some of the glory of Solomon's home and were doing so with the covetousness of Jehoahaz. Whatever the Jews' motives were, we know that while they primped their houses, the temple was unfinished. Therefore, God asked the Jews to take a long look inside their hearts (Haggai 1:5). By giving them a synopsis of their current predicament, he helped them to honestly evaluate what they saw.

Honest Evaluation

7. Read Haggai 1:6 and 9–11. What became of the Israelites' efforts to live comfortable lives?

8. Read Haggai 1:8. Compare the reasons God wanted the temple built with the reasons the Jews built cedar-paneled houses.

Zechariah's prophesying was less bone-chilling than Haggai's, but it was just as powerful. He urged the Jews to avoid the sins of their ancestors and to heed the Lord (Zechariah 1:3–6). He gave Zerubbabel this encouraging message: "Not by might, nor by power, but by my spirit, saith the LORD of hosts" (4:6). In other words, God's power, not mankind's ability, was the impetus to carry out His will. Further, Zechariah shared the wonderful news that the Lord would use Zerubbabel to finish the temple. The Lord revealed, "The hands of Zerubbabel have laid the foundation of this house; his hands shall also finish it; and thou shalt know that the LORD of hosts hath sent me unto you" (v. 9).

9. Read Ezra 5:1 and 2 and Haggai 1:12. How did Zerubbabel and Jeshua respond to the prophets' challenges?

10. Review Haggai 1:6–11. What do you think motivated the Jews the most to respond positively to the prophets' challenges?

Political Opposition

The rebuilding of the temple mentioned in Ezra 5:2 began in 520 BC, the second year of the reign of Darius, king of Persia (4:24). By putting a construction team back on the job at the temple site, Zerubbabel and Jeshua bothered the Devil. Without hesitation, an official delegation arrived to ask if the Jews had a building permit. "Who hath commanded you to build this house, and to make up this wall?" they inquired (5:3).

The delegates were Tatnai and Shethar-Boznai. Tatnai governed the area west of the Euphrates. Shethar-Boznai may have been his secretary or assistant, and the "companions" must have been lower-ranking officials. Like any political commission, they knew how to ask questions. They asked the Jews who had authorized them to build the temple, and they requested the builders' names (vv. 3, 4).

11. According to Ezra 5:5, why did the opposition fail to halt the construction of the temple?

12. Read 1 Peter 3:12. Where does the Lord center His focus today?

13. How should this truth encourage believers to continue serving Him?

Unable to halt the temple's construction, Tatnai and his associates wrote to King Darius (Ezra 5:6). To their credit, they didn't falsely accuse the Jews; they simply reported the facts and asked the king to search his records to ascertain whether or not the Jews had been authorized to build the temple (vv. 7–17). We learn from this letter that construction of the temple was proceeding at a vigorous pace. Huge stones and timber had been placed into the walls, prompting Tatnai to advise Darius, "This work goeth fast on, and prospereth in their hands" (v. 8). Obviously, encouraged by God's prophets and His providential protection, the Jews were overcoming every obstacle to complete the temple. We also learn from this letter what the builders believed about themselves and about God.

14. Read Ezra 5:11. Identify what the Jews recognized about themselves.

15. Describe what the Jews acknowledged about God.

The Jews related the decree that Cyrus gave them to rebuild the temple. This decree was written on a scroll and stored in Persia. A search of the records there would reveal that the Jews were telling the truth. The officials requested that the king have the records searched to verify the Jews' claims.

Political Support

Darius decreed such a search of the royal archives (Ezra 6:1). It revealed that Cyrus had prescribed the building of the temple in Jerusalem and had restored to the Jews the vessels Nebuchadnezzar had taken from it in 586 BC (vv. 2–5). Armed with this data, Darius wrote to Tatnai. His letter issued a restraining order to Tatnai and his associates (vv. 6, 7). He gave additional orders that must have made Tatnai bristle when he read them.

16. Read Ezra 6:8–10. What additional orders did Darius issue to Tatnai and his allies?

17. According to verses 11 and 12, what warning did Darius issue?

18. Describe the effect Darius's letter must have had on the Jews.

19. What evidence have you witnessed that showed that God opposes those who oppose His servants?

It didn't take Tatnai and his associates long to swing into action. Ezra 6:13 informs us that they speedily carried out the king's decree. After all, their jobs and even their lives were on the line. No one but a self-destructive fool would have defied Darius. This welcome turn of events and the faithful prophesying of Haggai and Zechariah kept the workers' morale high. They completed their work in the sixth year of Darius's reign, 515 BC (vv. 14, 15).

Making It Personal

We should not expect to be exempt from opposition when we serve the Lord. It is inevitable, but "we are more than conquerors through him that loved us" (Romans 8:37). We must not give up, but always look up to the Lord for grace and strength. He will not fail us. He expects us to do His work, and He enables us to do His work.

20. Read 1 Corinthians 15:58, and evaluate your work for the Lord. Is it steady and consistent?

21. What reasons do you have to remain active in the work of the Lord?

22. How will you improve your Christian work record this week?

23. Memorize 1 Corinthians 15:58.

Dedicated to God

*True dedication to God involves sacrifice
and separation from sin.*

Ezra 6:16–22

"I beseech you therefore, brethren, by the mercies of God, that ye present your bodies a living sacrifice, holy, acceptable unto God, which is your reasonable service. And be not conformed to this world: but be ye transformed by the renewing of your mind, that ye may prove what is that good, and acceptable, and perfect, will of God" (Romans 12:1, 2).

Life seems to be a succession of celebrations. We celebrate birthdays, national holidays, graduations, weddings, job promotions, anniversaries, and even weight loss. Such celebrations are always joyful. Good food, good friends, good moods, and good memories abound. Most celebrations last several hours or all day, although some extend for a weekend or even a week. Celebrations are not unique to our era, of course; they have always been a part of history. Undoubtedly they will continue into eternity. In Heaven we will celebrate our redemption and the glory of the Lamb that was slain (Revelation 4; 5).

As we will see, the repatriated Jews celebrated the completion of the temple in Jerusalem.

Getting Started

1. What is your favorite celebration of the year?

2. What do you do to prepare for that celebration?

Searching the Scriptures

Dedication Day

After a decade and a half of battling discouragement and legal delays, the Jews finally completed the house of God and dedicated it to Him. All Israel—the priests, the Levites, and the rest of the repatriated Jews—celebrated the dedication of the temple. God had brought them back to the Promised Land and had enabled them to build His house there.

3. Read Ezra 6:16. Write a definition of "dedicate." Use a dictionary if necessary.

4. By inference, what promise concerning themselves were the Jews making to God when they dedicated the temple?

5. With what emotion did they make that promise?

The finished temple meant the Jews had opened a new door of opportunity. They could finally begin implementing God's instructions about His house. By dedicating the temple, the Jews were communicating to God their personal dedication to obeying His instructions. In that sense, their dedication of the temple actually had more to do with them than it did the temple, for the temple was worthless if the Jews weren't dedicated to using it as God had specifically prescribed in His Word.

The idea of dedicating oneself to God is even more evident in the New Testament Epistles. The believer, not any church building, is called the temple of God in the Epistles. First Corinthians 3:16 identifies believers corporately as "the temple of God," and 1 Corinthians 6:19 identifies the believer's body as "the temple of the Holy Ghost." Ephesians 2:22 addresses believers—saved Jews and saved Gentiles—as "an habitation of God through the Spirit."

6. Read 1 Corinthians 6:19 and 20. Identify what God expects believers, His temples, to dedicate themselves to today.

Making Sacrifices

Sacrifices accompanied the dedication of the temple. The Jews offered one hundred bullocks, two hundred rams, four hundred lambs, and twelve male goats as a sin offering for all Israel (Ezra 6:17). The twelve male goats represented the twelve tribes of Israel. Some people insist that the Assyrian captivity obliterated the identification of Israel's ten northern tribes. They theorize what may have happened to the "ten lost tribes of Israel." Nevertheless, God knows the tribal identity of every Jew, and in the Tribulation He will seal twelve thousand from each of Israel's twelve tribes (Revelation 7:4).

7. Read Ezra 6:17. What were the Jews demonstrating by voluntarily offering sacrifices at the dedication of the temple?

8. What are some characteristics of a sacrifice?

9. Read Romans 12:1. What does it mean for a believer to offer him- or herself as a "living sacrifice"?

True dedication involves sacrifice. The Jews demonstrated their dedication to God through voluntarily offering animal sacrifices. Today believers still make sacrifices to God, but not animal sacrifices. Christ's final sacrifice on the cross did away with animal sacrifices to cover sin and to demonstrate dedication.

10. What sacrifices can a dedicated believer make to God? (See Philippians 4:12 and 13, Romans 12:1 and 2, Ephesians 5:15 and 16, and 2 Corinthians 9:6 and 7.)

A small city allocated thousands of dollars to the building and equipping of an additional fire station. Months later, the new station gained the admiration of the entire community. Its proud structure, gleaming fire engines, and rescue vehicles inspired the citizens' confidence in their elected officials, and the elected officials could hardly wait to hold a public dedication of the new facility. Then someone set the officials back on their heels by observing that it might be best to delay the dedication. You see, in all the hoopla surrounding the building and equipment, the officials had neglected to hire any firefighters to operate the station.

The builders of Zerubbabel's temple didn't make that mistake. Taking directions from the law of Moses, they assigned priests and Levites to serve in the temple (Ezra 6:18). They followed the pattern of "divisions" and "courses" that David had set for those who would minister in the Lord's house (1 Chronicles 23:1–6; 24:1). There was enough work for all, so everyone would have an opportunity for service.

Purification

The Israelites observed the very first Passover in anticipation of imminent deliverance from bondage in Egypt. Hundreds of years later the Jews observed the Passover again after the Lord had delivered them from captivity in Babylon. They obeyed the Word of God by observing it "upon the fourteenth day of the first month" (Ezra 6:19; Exodus 12:6, 14).

11. What did the priests do before participating in the observance of the Passover (Ezra 6:19, 20)?

True dedication demands purity and holiness. God wanted the Jews to keep the Passover, but only if the priests were properly purified. God has no interest in sacrifices offered from "dirty hands."

12. Read Zechariah 3:1–5. How did God vividly portray His demand that Joshua the high priest be purified before serving in God's newly constructed temple?

While believers today can claim that the blood of Christ has cleansed them from all sin, their hands and their clothes still get "dirty" when they sin. God wants us, as a royal priesthood, to be blameless as we serve Him. If we are truly dedicated to God, we will take seriously God's desire for us to be holy as He is holy.

13. Read 1 Peter 1:14–16 and 2:9–12. Record what Peter wrote about the need for believers to live holy lives before God.

14. What simple provision for a believer's sin did God give in 1 John 1:9?

Fellowship and Joy

After purifying themselves, the priests and Levites prepared the passover lambs for all the Jews, for their fellow priests, and for themselves (Ezra 6:20). The returnees and those who had never left the land but had separated themselves from the heathen practices of their Gentile neighbors observed the Passover together (v. 21).

15. Read Ezra 6:21. What potential tensions might have cropped up between the returnees and the Jews who had never left the land?

16. For what reason did the Jews who had never left the land separate themselves from the filth of the nations?

When God's people have a mutual dedication, they also enjoy fellowship. If the Jews who were never taken into captivity hadn't separated themselves from the filth of the nations around them, their relationship with the returnees wouldn't have been harmonious. In fact, their relationship would have been hostile. Ezra 4:4 and 5 record the hostility the Jews who chose to follow pagan gods had toward the returnees.

The original passover procedure required the selecting of an unblemished male lamb or kid of the first year for each household, shedding its blood, smearing its blood on the doorposts, roasting the entire lamb in fire, and eating all of it that night with unleavened bread and bitter herbs. If any of the lamb remained uneaten, it was to be burned (Exodus 12:3–10).

Paul wrote in 1 Corinthians 5:7 that "Christ our passover is sacrificed for us." Like Israel's passover lamb, Jesus was unblemished. He never had a sinful thought or performed a sinful deed. Peter wrote that we were redeemed "with the precious blood of Christ, as of a lamb without blemish and without spot" (1 Peter 1:19).

Just as Israel's Passover reminded the Israelites that God had delivered them from slavery in Egypt, so Christians ought to remember that Christ redeemed us with His blood from a life of slavery to sin. Writing to the Romans, Paul testified, "But God be thanked, that ye were the servants of sin, but ye have obeyed from the heart that form of doctrine which was delivered you. Being then made free from sin, ye became the servants of righteousness" (Romans 6:17, 18).

After observing the Passover on the fourteenth day of the first month, Israel kept the Feast of Unleavened Bread for seven days, as the law of Moses instructed (Exodus 12:15; Leviticus 23:6–8). Since the Bible often refers to leaven as a picture of sin, which begins small but increases dramatically, this feast gave the Children of Israel a visual reminder that the Lord demanded their purity and separation.

17. Read Ezra 6:22. What did the Lord do for the Jews who had purified themselves?

True and lasting satisfaction in life comes from God alone. This statement has always been true. Dedicate yourself to God, and He will meet your needs (Matthew 6:33). All of life is a celebration when first we dedicate ourselves to God. Want to celebrate life? Truly give yourself to God.

Making It Personal

18. Would a close friend or your spouse characterize your life as dedicated to God? What evidence might he or she cite to support that conclusion?

19. Have you dedicated yourself as a living sacrifice to God? Check the following indicators of dedication that are evident in your life.

❑ I am a baptized member of my church.

❑ I am serving in my church.

❑ I have indicated to God that I will go and do whatever He desires.

❑ I make spending time with God a priority.

❑ I purposefully look for opportunities to give financially to God's work.

❑ I purposefully look for opportunities to serve others.

❑ I take care of my sin immediately.

❑ I have a pure thought-life.

❑ I get along with others.

❑ I have joy regardless of my circumstances.

Every believer can say his or her dedication to God can go deeper. But that isn't an excuse to be satisfied with where you are in your Christian life.

20. Over what area of your life does God not yet have control? Write a prayer of dedication to God, committing that area of your life to Him.

21. Memorize Romans 12:1 and 2. Resolve to make these verses characteristic of your life.

Lesson 6

Traveling with Guidebook in Hand

God's Word is the believer's guide for life.

Ezra 7

"For Ezra had prepared his heart to seek the law of the LORD, and to do it, and to teach in Israel statutes and judgments" (Ezra 7:10).

Planning on visiting Morocco? Most of us never will. But just in case you do, here's a tip from an experienced traveler: "We highly recommend taking a guide to the desert because if you don't have a Land Rover it's really difficult to drive on your own with a normal car. You don't have the experience and the car could break down in the middle of nowhere. Guides know how to drive a normal car and they know where the big stones under the dunes are" (Carmen Gomez Aparicio, "Moving About," *Morocco,* www.lonelyplanet.com/letters/afr/morpc.htm). Tourists who head into the Moroccan desert without a guide are likely headed for trouble.

In a sense, life is like a trip through a Moroccan desert. Pitfalls and hidden dangers are everywhere. Even believers can't travel successfully through life without a guide. God gave the Bible to mankind to serve as the guide for life. The Bible is a gift and should be cherished and studied fervently.

Getting Started

1. Describe a time when you were in a new place and in desperate need of a guide.

2. When have you most felt the need for a guide for your life?

3. What do you see as evidence that people live as if they are wandering through a desert without a guide?

Searching the Scriptures

To understand Ezra's contribution to Jewish history, we need to review some of Persia's fifth-century history. From 485 to 465 BC, Xerxes ruled Persia. This powerful king quelled rebellions in Babylon and Egypt and invaded Greece. Athens fell to Xerxes, but later the Persian king's thrill of victory turned to the agony of defeat when his fleet lost one-third of its ships to the Greeks in a battle at Salamis. In subsequent years the Greeks routed the Persians from Europe and forced them to withdraw their ships from the Aegean Sea. Xerxes' reign ended when one of his nobles, Artabanus, assassinated Xerxes and elevated his third son, Artaxerxes I Longimanus, to the throne. Artaxerxes put his brother Darius to death, killed Artabanus, and stripped his other brother, Hystaspes, of his power as satrap (governor) of Bactria. In 460 BC Egypt rebelled, siding with Greece against Persia.

Conditions in Judah, too, were less than ideal around 460 BC. The Jews had become apathetic. They had settled into a pattern of lifeless worship; they were neglecting the law; and some of them had married unbelieving Gentiles.

God used the conditions facing Persia to persuade Artaxerxes to let Ezra lead a delegation to Judah. Artaxerxes may have reasoned that such kindness on his part would win the favor of the Jews' God and keep Egypt at bay.

The words "now after these things" (Ezra 7:1) bridge almost sixty years, from the closing events of Ezra 6 to those of Ezra 7. In the seventh year of his reign, Artaxerxes granted Ezra permission to lead a second group of Jews from Babylon to Jerusalem.

Skilled in God's Word

A member of the Aaronic priestly line, Ezra had descended from Aaron through such notable priests as Phinehas, Zadok, and Hilkiah (Ezra 7:1–5). But his heritage didn't automatically make him acceptable before God. Ezra knew that God would be pleased with him only as he devoted himself to God's Word.

4. Read Ezra 7:6. What does it take to become skilled in God's Word?

Ezra noted that the law of Moses was "given" by God (v. 6). Essentially Ezra saw God's Word as a gift from God.

5. How does a person treat God's Word when he or she views it as a gift from God rather than as a list of rules?

6. What apparent difference did believing that God's Word is a gift make in Ezra's life (v. 6)?

It took courage for Ezra to approach Artaxerxes and ask him if he could lead a delegation back to Israel. But God's hand was on Ezra, who had become sensitive to the Lord's leading through God's Word.

7. Why is a person who ignores God's Word not likely to attempt something great for the Lord?

According to the list of returnees, 1,773 men accompanied Ezra on the nine-hundred-mile journey from Babylon to Jerusalem (Ezra 8). The group included "some of the children of Israel, and of the priests, and the Levites, and the singers, and the porters, and the Nethinims" (7:7). The priests belonged to the family of Aaron in the tribe of Levi, whereas the Levites were the rest of the members of the tribe of Levi. The singers were Levites who provided music for temple worship, and the porters were Levites with duties defined in 1 Chronicles 26:1–19. Lowest in the order of those who served in the temple were the Nethinims, probably slaves who performed menial tasks.

Ezra's group of exiles took four months to trek the nine hundred miles to Jerusalem (Ezra 7:8, 9). This means that Ezra's group traveled approximately eight miles a day, six days a week, for four months. With a walking speed that probably averaged two miles per hour, the group would have walked about four hours a day.

8. Imagine taking the trip with Ezra. How would you hold up?

9. Read Ezra 7:9. What enabled Ezra's group to successfully make the trip?

Prepared Heart

Ezra faced an enormous challenge in Jerusalem. The people of Israel had sunk into apathy, and only a mighty pull by the Holy Spirit would lift them out of it. Ezra's message to the people would have to be Spirit authored and Spirit focused. Ezra would have to teach God's Word faithfully and forcefully by precept and example. Thankfully, he had prepared well for this challenge.

10. According to Ezra 7:10, how had Ezra prepared for the challenge of reviving God's people?

"Seek" in verse 10 includes the idea of frequenting. Ezra didn't take a casual approach to God's Word. He studied and meditated on it until he understood it. In preparing his heart, Ezra must have humbled himself before God and acknowledged that he needed a guide for life. His preparation must also have included a decision to love God's Word.

11. Read Psalm 1:1 and 2. What decisions by Ezra are reflected in these verses?

12. What promise does God make to those who, like Ezra, prepare their hearts to spend time in His Word?

Obedience

Ezra had prepared his heart not only to seek the law of the Lord, but also to do it (Ezra 7:10). Who wants to be told what to do by someone who doesn't practice what he preaches? The Jews in Judah could observe God's truth in Ezra's daily conduct. They could see that Ezra lived what he taught. The pattern Ezra followed—seek, do, and teach—never goes out of style, and it serves every Christian well because each of us is a teacher.

When Ezra reached Jerusalem, he carried the Word of the King of Heaven and earth in one hand and a letter from the King of Persia in his other hand. As we read Ezra 7:11–26, which quotes Artaxerxes' words, we learn that the king of Persia respected Ezra as a man of God and gave him extensive authority for his work in Jerusalem. He identified Ezra as a priest and a teacher of God's commandments and statutes

(vv. 11, 12). He also described Ezra as having the Law of God in his hand (v. 14).

13. Read Ezra 7:14. What did Artaxerxes communicate about Ezra by describing him as having the law of God in his hand?

Ezra's tool was the Word of God. He loved it, trusted it, depended on it, and eventually used it to help God's people in Israel. As Ezra taught God's Word, it guided God's people, much as Moses' staff guided the Children of Israel through the wilderness to the Promised Land.

14. What can a believer do to keep his or her guidebook for life, God's Word, in hand?

The King's Letter

Artaxerxes allowed all the Jews in his empire to accompany Ezra to Jerusalem if they wanted to do so (7:13). He and his seven counselors (his cabinet members) donated silver and gold for the Lord's work in Jerusalem, and they encouraged others to contribute to the fund (vv. 14–16). Artaxerxes wanted Ezra to have sufficient funds to buy all the animals and supplies he needed to perform the sacrifices required by the law of Moses (v. 17). He let Ezra decide how to allocate the excess funds (v. 18), and gave him utensils for the temple (v. 19). Furthermore, he opened an account for Ezra at the king's treasure house, allowing him to withdraw nearly four tons of silver, six hundred bushels of wheat, six hundred gallons of wine, six hundred gallons of olive oil, and an unlimited supply of salt (vv. 20–22).

Artaxerxes ordered all his treasurers "beyond the river" (west of the Euphrates) to cooperate fully with Ezra by giving him whatever he requested for the temple (v. 21). The king of Persia didn't want to offend the God of Heaven and incur His wrath (v. 23). The Greeks and Egyptians were supplying him with more than enough trouble as it was. He also ordered the treasurers not to impose any taxes on the priests, Levites, singers, porters, Nethinim, or servants of God's temple (v. 24).

Finally, the king's letter authorized Ezra to establish a judicial system in Judah and to teach God's laws to all the Jews (v. 25). Those who refused to comply with God's laws were to be judged.

15. Read Ezra 7:26. What punishments did Artaxerxes decree should be carried out against those who refused to observe God's law?

16. Read Ezra 7:27. What made Artaxerxes so interested in the obedience of the Jews in Jerusalem?

Ezra's Gratitude

With his heart overflowing with gratitude, Ezra praised the Lord that His hand upon him had given him courage. Knowing that the Lord was directing his steps, Ezra had assembled leaders from Israel to accompany him to Jerusalem (v. 28).

17. Read Ezra 7:28. Why is it significant that Ezra mentioned God's mercy? What was Ezra trying to communicate about himself? What was Ezra trying to communicate about God?

Obviously God had opened all the right doors for Ezra. Today, too, He opens all the right doors for those who prepare their hearts to seek His Word. Our responsibility is to treasure the Word of God and trust the God of the Word. Because He is the dependable, omnipotent, and merciful Heavenly Father, He will not disappoint us!

Making It Personal

Whatever you do for the Lord should flow from a heart prepared to seek God's Word, to obey it, and to teach it.

18. How have you prepared your heart to seek God's Word this week? Have you humbled yourself by recognizing that you can't traverse the wilderness of life without the Bible as your guide? If not, do so now.

19. Do something to deepen your study of God's Word this week. Here are some suggestions.

- Buy a good study Bible.

- Take advantage of Web sites that offer free basic study tools. Try Biblegateway.com and Blueletterbible.org for starters.

- Investigate purchasing Bible study software.

- Purchase commentaries and other Bible study books to use as references. Consider the following:

  The Bible Knowledge Commentary (2-volume set)
  The Bible Exposition Commentary (6-volume set)
  The Moody Atlas of Bible Lands
  The New Unger's Bible Dictionary

- Keep a stack of verse cards with you to memorize and meditate on as time allows.

20. Plan to share what you learn from God's Word this week. If you have a testimony time at your church, be ready to tell others what God has taught you from His Word. Otherwise, tell your spouse or a friend or someone who needs to be encouraged by what you learned.

21. Memorize Ezra 7:10 and purpose to follow Ezra's example.

A Journey without Incident

God is dependable.

Ezra 8

"Behold, I am the LORD, the God of all flesh: is there any thing too hard for me?" (Jeremiah 32:27).

Jim takes his two little dogs—a Maltese and a toy poodle—for a walk every day. They seem to enjoy the walk, but occasionally Molly and Rosie drag a little, especially when they reach a distant point from home. But when Jim asks, "Do you want to go home?" they quickly turn around and gain a burst of energy. Instead of lagging behind Jim, they break into a fast pace, pulling him in the direction of home.

Something similar happens when Jim takes Molly and Rosie to their groomer. They know the route, so the closer they get to the groomer, the louder they cry. But when Jim picks them up after the grooming, puts them in the car, and says, "We're going home," they sit quietly all the way home.

It seems that even dogs realize there is no place like home.

Getting Started

1. What makes your home a special place?

2. When have you been traveling and feared you might not make it home?

Searching the Scriptures

The List of Exiles

When Ezra called for volunteers to return to Jerusalem from Babylon, he wasn't overwhelmed with applicants. Only a small number of Jews signed up for the long journey. Probably many Jews in Babylon had grown accustomed to life there. They had built houses and planted gardens and were earning a living. Why would they exchange familiar surroundings and a comfortable lifestyle for an uncertain future?

The list of families in Ezra 8:2–14 serves as an honor roll commemorating the daring faith and love for God that characterized those who accompanied Ezra from Babylon in the reign of Artaxerxes (v. 1). Apparently faith and devotion run deep and long in some families, because the major families that appear in this list also appear in Zerubbabel's list of returnees (2:3–15). Only the name Joab in 8:9 was absent from the earlier list.

The names of priestly and Davidic families appear first in the list of returning exiles (Ezra 8:2, 3). Altogether, about seventeen hundred men and their families joined Ezra's expedition, including the Levites and Nethinim who joined the expedition late. Three months and eighteen days later they would arrive in Jerusalem. (See 7:9.)

Recruiting Levites

Ezra gathered the exiles together by the Ahava Canal. Probably the canal flowed through the Ahava district near Babylon and into the

Euphrates River. The assembled exiles camped by the canal for three days. This encampment gave Ezra sufficient time to count the people and prepare them for the long journey to Jerusalem. If anyone had second thoughts about making the trip, this three-day stop gave them ample opportunity to go home. But no one deserted!

When Ezra surveyed who was in the camp, he found no Levites. This absence was a problem, since the Levites were integral to the spiritual life of the nation. Other Levites were already in Jerusalem, but the main focus of Ezra's return was spiritual reform. If not one single Levite was willing to return with Ezra, he would have a hard time communicating the importance of God's Word and His temple. Teaching God's law to the exiles in Judah required the Levites' help.

3. Read Ezra 8:15. How could Ezra have reacted to not finding any Levites among the people?

4. Read Ezra 8:16 and 17. What did Ezra do to solve the problem of having no Levites in his group of returnees?

5. What do you suppose Ezra told his recruiters to tell the Levites of Casiphia?

God gave the recruiters success; 38 Levites and 220 Nethinim enlisted for service in Jerusalem (vv. 18–20). Ezra wrote that the team brought Levites to the camp "by the good hand of our God upon us" (v. 18). Initially the Levites may have resisted the call to serve because the prominent positions in Jerusalem had been filled. The reasons that had kept the Levites in Babylon, whatever those reasons were, fell apart when God placed His hand on them.

Fasting and Prayer

6. Read Ezra 8:21. Why did Ezra proclaim a fast at the river of Ahava?

7. If you had been one of Ezra's advisors, what would you have told Ezra when he proclaimed a fast on the eve of leaving on a long, arduous journey?

Together Ezra and his countrymen placed themselves, their children, and their goods in God's hands (v. 21). By fasting they were telling God that they were serious about wanting His help. They were carrying tons of silver and gold and other goods and supplies. A band of thieves could easily take their lives and steal their lightly guarded goods. (See verse 31.) The returnees laid aside their fear and pride and humbly acknowledged that God had to lead them if their journey was going to be a success.

8. Read Ezra 8:22. Why didn't Ezra ask Artaxerxes for a military escort?

Thirteen years after Ezra's return, Nehemiah requested a military escort for his journey to Jerusalem. But Ezra had believed that such a request would weaken God's testimony. So the returnees turned their concerns over to God, and He honored their faith. God communicated to the group that they could depend on Him and take the trip in peace (v. 23).

9. Describe a time when you laid aside your own attempts to solve a problem and depended on God for a solution.

10. What happened as a result?

Wisely, Ezra delegated responsibility for getting the gold and silver, offerings, and temple articles to Jerusalem. He selected twelve chief priests and twelve Levites and delivered the treasures to them. No one could accuse Ezra of siphoning funds into his own pockets. Nor could they accuse him of keeping poor financial records. He weighed, counted, and recorded the gold and silver, the offerings, and the vessels. Then he instructed the twenty-four appointees to take their responsibility seriously. He reminded them that they themselves and the vessels were "holy unto the LORD" (v. 28). He explained, "The silver and the gold are a freewill offering unto the LORD God of your fathers." He commanded the appointees to guard the treasures until they delivered them to the leaders of the Jews in Jerusalem. The appointed priests and Levites took custody of the treasures before breaking camp to begin the difficult trek to Jerusalem (vv. 24–30).

Departure and Arrival

11. Read Ezra 8:31. What did God do for the returnees?

In a matter-of-fact way, verse 31 states what God did for the returnees. The plainness of the account supports the truth that when God keeps His word to those who depend on Him, it's not something rare and uncommon. In fact it is rather ordinary. Of course the Jews would be safe! They were depending on the God of the universe.

12. Read Jeremiah 32:27. What rhetorical question did God ask?

13. What circumstances for believers often seem too hard for God?

14. When have you seen God do something awesome in your life? Was it hard not to be at least a little surprised or stunned when He answered your prayer?

15. Read Acts 12:1–16. How did the believers who were praying for Peter respond when he showed up at their prayer meeting?

In his *Notes on Ezra, Nehemiah, and Esther*, H. A. Ironside commented that, based on Jewish tradition, many believe Ezra and the returnees sang Psalms 120—134 at various stages of their four-month journey. These psalms focus on the joy of worshiping the Lord in His holy temple.

Three days of rest greeted the exiles when they reached Jerusalem. Undoubtedly the returnees welcomed the opportunity that brief period gave them to relax and refresh both soul and body. They would need renewed energy for the work ahead.

When the exiles' three-day rest concluded, the twelve priests and twelve Levites delivered the treasures they had transported from Babylon. Everything was carefully weighed and recorded in the presence of those who would take custody of it (Ezra 8:33, 34). As good stewards, they had followed excellent accounting procedures in receiving and depositing the treasures.

Worship at the Temple

Displaying national unity, the returnees expressed their devotion to the Lord by offering twelve bullocks, ninety-six rams, seventy-seven lambs, and twelve male goats (v. 35). This was their first occasion of worship at the rebuilt temple in their native land. It must have been a joyful and deeply significant spiritual experience.

The returnees also delivered copies of Artaxerxes' decree to the satraps in the region. This communication brought a gratifying response: the officials provided assistance and supported the Jews' worship (v. 36).

Although the Jews rejoiced in their safe journey, they had work to do in rebuilding Jerusalem and dealing with the spiritual decline of those already in the land. Ezra would need spiritual resolve and strength from God in dealing with the problems. God, of course, would give him all he needed to carry out his ministry.

Making It Personal

The decision to leave Babylon must have been difficult for many Jews. After all, they were born in Babylon and knew nothing of Jerusalem. They were familiar with Babylon, and their livelihood was there. A long journey over rough terrain to Jerusalem would not appeal to them—unless they were men and women of faith. They had to believe that God was leading them and that they could depend on Him to provide for them on the journey and in Jerusalem.

16. Examine your life. What facts indicate that you might be depending on yourself rather than God?

❏ I worry about what might happen to me or my loved ones.

❏ I make my decisions without consulting God.

❏ I don't pray about my problems.

❏ I try to manipulate people.

❏ I try to do everything myself.

❏

❏

❏

17. Humble prayer is the first step in becoming dependent on God. Read Ezra 8:21 again. Write a prayer to God expressing your humble dependence on Him.

18. What additional steps can you take toward developing dependence on God?

19. Memorize Jeremiah 32:27. Quote the verse every time you are tempted to doubt God and to depend on yourself instead.

Lesson 8

Rebellion and Revival

God is gracious and merciful.

Ezra 9; 10

"The sacrifices of God are a broken spirit: a broken and a contrite heart, O God, thou wilt not despise" (Psalm 51:17).

April 13, 1992, was a busy, frustrating day in Chicago's history. Water from the Chicago River poured into an underground freight tunnel beneath the Loop, the center of downtown Chicago. Later that day, electricity to numerous buildings in the Loop was shut down, forcing office buildings, stores, and restaurants to close. Thousands of employees, dismissed from work by 2:00 p.m., scrambled to find transportation home. Even the Chicago Board of Trade, the city's financial nerve center, closed. Before long, forty feet of water flooded some subbasements, and questions flooded the minds of city officials and members of the media. How did it happen? Who is responsible? How can we stop the leak and get rid of the water? How long will Loop buildings be without electricity? When will the city return to normal?

A dredging company hired to replace a group of log pilings in the Chicago River drove new pilings a few feet from the old. Apparently one log penetrated a weak freight tunnel wall, and the river poured in.

An early investigation disclosed that a few city employees had known for weeks that the tunnel wall had deteriorated and was leaking. It would have cost about fifty thousand dollars to repair the initial

damage, but no one issued a work order. When the flood hit, the estimated cost of damage soared beyond millions of dollars.

In Ezra's day, a sin emerged that threatened to flood Israel and
drown the people in idolatry and immorality. As Israel's spiritual leader,
Ezra could have ignored the sin, but he chose to confront it. By doing
so, he led Israel in a revival that saved it from permanent and costly
spiritual damage.

Getting Started

1. What costly damage have you known to result because of human
error or unwillingness to spend a little money to fix the problem in its
early stage?

2. How might prompt church discipline avert a spiritual disaster?

Searching the Scriptures

Reports of Intermarriage

Certain leaders in Israel reported to Ezra that the people of Israel,
the priests, and the Levites had not separated themselves from their
heathen neighbors (Ezra 9:1). The offending Jews were practicing idolatry and its accompanying sins. Furthermore, they had married heathen
women. Making a bad situation worse, Israel's leaders were the chief
offenders (v. 2). Obviously they had ignored the lessons of history. In
Joshua's time, the Israelites who entered Canaan had a mandate from
God to expel the heathen tribes.

3. Read Numbers 33:51–53. What did the Lord tell the Israelites to do

    a. to the inhabitants of Canaan?

    b. to the inhabitants' pictures and molten images?

    c. to the inhabitants' high places?

4. Read Judges 3:5 and 6. What sinful relationships did the Israelites establish with the Canaanites?

5. Read 2 Chronicles 36:14–17. What calamity did Israel's evil ways ultimately bring on them?

After the Jews returned from the Captivity, they repeated the sins of former generations—sins that had ruined the nation.

Do you wonder how the repatriated exiles fell into such wickedness? Likely, as time passed, they gradually became comfortable with their heathen neighbors' lifestyle and worship. As the comfort level rose, the Jews erased more and more of the lines of separation between them and the heathen until finally the lines had disappeared.

Ezra's Response

6. Read Ezra 9:3 and 4. How did Ezra respond to the report about the sin in Israel?

The Jews had been burned when playing with fire. But they toyed with the flames again. This situation astonished Ezra. At the time of the evening sacrifice, he fell to his knees and extended his hands toward

Heaven (v. 5). Contritely identifying himself with the nation's sin, he confessed how ashamed he was.

7. Read Ezra 9:6 and 7. How did Ezra describe the Jews' guilt?

8. Why must admission of guilt before God be the first step in restoring fellowship with Him?

Ezra acknowledged that sin had blotted Israel's history and caused the Captivity (v. 7).

9. Read Ezra 9:8 and 9. God extended both grace and mercy to the captive Jews when He allowed them to return to the Promised Land. What is grace? What is mercy?

10. What do God's grace and mercy offer the believer today?

11. Describe a time when you experienced God's grace or mercy in your life.

Further, Ezra admitted that the remnant of Jews in the land had trampled God's mercy and grace. They used their return from Persia as an opportunity to sin. Their involvement with the heathen violated God's clear commands and therefore jeopardized the nation's existence (vv. 10–14).

12. Read Ezra 9:15. What truths did Ezra admit before God?

The People Cry out to God

Ezra's deep dismay about Israel's sin tugged at the hearts of a great many exiles. When he had prayed and confessed, "weeping and casting himself down before the house of God" (10:1), a large throng of men and women and children joined him. Their tears mingled with his. Ezra described the people as weeping "very sore."

Shechaniah, the son of Jehiel, gave everyone a reason to look up through their tears to see a ray of hope.

13. Read Ezra 10:2. What was the only source of hope for Israel? (See Psalm 130.)

14. Can a believer ever say that he or she is hopelessly caught in habitual sin? What would you say to a believer who claims, "I can't help sinning"?

Shechaniah counseled Ezra to tell the Jews to make a covenant with God to put away their foreign wives and the children of those marriages (v. 3). He promised Ezra full cooperation and advised him to "be of good courage, and do it" (v. 4).

15. How difficult would it have been for the Jews to put away their foreign wives and children?

16. How were the Jews' relationships with their foreign wives like a believer's relationship with his or her favorite sin?

Ezra's Proclamation

Encouraged by Shechaniah's words, Ezra followed a course of action. First he secured a pledge from the chief priests, the Levites, and the people that they would put away their wives (v. 5). Next he entered the chamber of Johanan, where he fasted and mourned Israel's transgression (v. 6). Then he issued a proclamation summoning all the exiles in Jerusalem and Judah to assemble in Jerusalem (v. 7). Anyone who failed to appear in Jerusalem within three days would forfeit all his possessions and be excommunicated from the rest of the exiles (v. 8).

All the men of Judah and Benjamin answered Ezra's summons. They sat in the street where the temple stood, and they trembled (v. 9). They shook in their sandals, not only because they feared God's judgment but also because a heavy rain was soaking them. The miserable weather matched the misery of soul their sin had caused.

Ezra addressed the trembling Jews. "Ye have transgressed, and have taken strange wives, to increase the trespass of Israel," he told them (v. 10). Then Ezra asked the Jews to confess their sin to God (v. 11).

17. Read Ezra 10:11. What else did Ezra ask the people to do?

18. Why does only confessing a sin not lead to victory over it?

19. What might a believer do to practically separate him- or herself from sin in the following situations?

a. A young man is struggling with Internet pornography.

b. A young lady is dating an unsaved man.

c. A woman is spending hours a week gossiping on the phone.

d. A man is struggling with an alcohol addiction.

Like Ezra, spiritual leaders must confront sin and call upon transgressors to forsake the evil. A careless attitude toward sin insults Scripture, weakens a church's testimony, and saps its spiritual vitality. The apostle Paul advised Timothy that in preaching the Word, he must "reprove" and "rebuke" (2 Timothy 4:2). Part of a preacher's responsibility is to afflict the comfortable as well as to comfort the afflicted.

Putting away the Foreign Wives

The congregation of Israel agreed to put away their heathen wives (Ezra 10:12), but they recognized that the process would stretch far beyond a few days. The driving, wintry rain would make outdoor hearings impractical, and it would take considerable time to hear the many cases (v. 13). The people suggested that the elders and judges in each community hear the cases by appointment (v. 14). Only four leaders opposed this suggestion (v. 15).

Ezra and other leaders began the painful process of hearing each case involving the marriage of an exile to a foreigner (v. 16). They took about three months to judge the cases (v. 17). When the process ended, seventeen priests (vv. 18–22), ten Levites (vv. 23, 24), and eighty-four other Jews had been found guilty of marrying heathen women.

Making It Personal

Every believer desperately needs God's grace and mercy to live a holy, separated life. Without God's grace and mercy, a believer will continue to struggle with sin.

20. Praise God for His grace and mercy that brought you salvation.

21. Humbly confess any sin with which you have been struggling, and communicate to God your reliance on His grace to help you be victorious.

22. Put into action your trust in God's grace by taking steps to separate yourself from any besetting sin. List the steps here.

23. Memorize Psalm 51:17.

Behind the Scenes Preparation

The eye of faith sees the hand of God providentially at work.

Esther 1:1—2:20

"And we know that all things work together for good to them that love God, to them who are the called according to his purpose" (Romans 8:28).

On Thursday, June 13, 1991, a first printing of the Declaration of Independence was sold at an auction for 2.42 million dollars. The amazing thing about this document, however, was not the shock of its selling price but the location of its discovery. You see, the man who sold it at auction had purchased it at a flea market for only four dollars! The document was hidden behind the canvas of a cheap painting to which he took a liking. But after a close examination, which prompted him to peel back the canvas, he found this copy of the Declaration of Independence. What a find! It had been totally hidden yet ever present behind the picture.

As you read about that fantastic discovery, you might think, "Why doesn't that ever happen to me?" Imagine how exciting it would be to uncover something of such extraordinary value in such an unassuming place. It could even be life-changing!

A life-changing discovery is in store for you as you embark on your journey through ancient Persia with the book of Esther as your travel guide. This literary escort will lead you into the palace of a Persian king, and from that vantage point it will peel back the canvas of history to reveal the King of Kings—totally hidden yet ever present. In the unassuming events of life God is at work. He is there. What a find—to discover God Himself and His involvement in our daily lives! So don't head off to the flea market. Hook up with the book of Esther. Peel back the cover and discover this God of mystery. He is the sovereign of history and the guarantor of victory.

Getting Started

1. What is the most unexpected discovery you have ever made?

2. When have you sensed God's sovereign hand working behind the scenes of your life?

Searching the Scriptures

The God of Mystery

We begin with a question that might surprise you: Is God really here in the book of Esther? But we are not the first to ask it. The veracity and authenticity of the book of Esther has been questioned throughout history. Jewish and Christian scholars alike have questioned the appropriateness of this book's inclusion in the canon of Scripture. Their desire to dismiss Esther is based upon a variety of troubling discoveries. Consider a few of the findings.

The hero and heroine of the account, though showing great moral courage and national commitment at a time of real crisis, gave no evidence of having a genuine heart for God and His program. Mordecai and Esther were far from the Promised Land and, unlike Ezra, showed no concern to return. Esther showed little regard for obedience to the law as she willingly entered the harem of a Gentile king. Unlike Daniel, she showed no regard for the dietary regulations of the law as she partook of nonkosher foods and participated in the customs of a pagan culture (Esther 2:8–10). Both Mordecai and Esther chose to conceal their nationality and hide their Jewishness, unlike both Nehemiah and Daniel. Their conduct, though courageous in a crisis, was contrary to that of an obedient, God-fearing Old Testament believer.

Further objection arises from the fact that the book does not mention or show concern for the major tenets and institutions of Judaism that run throughout the rest of the Old Testament. Although a Gentile king is mentioned numerous times, Jehovah has nothing to do with the account. Or so it would appear.

However, these concerns that cause some to question the authenticity of Esther actually serve to accomplish the opposite. Though most of Israel did not return to the Promised Land and had no regard for God's theocratic program centered in that land, God had not forgotten or abandoned them. He did not forget His covenant with Abraham. In His providence He watched over them and delivered them because He is faithful to His promises.

Though the main Actor is never mentioned, the eye of faith sees Him center stage. He dominates the drama. He has the lead role. In fact, God is not only the principal actor, but also the divine director and the sovereign screenwriter. He wrote the script, though He doesn't appear in the credits. He gives the cues, though He never appears on stage. Certainly the dominating theme and message of this drama is "God is in control." He is ever present, accomplishing His purpose of delivering His people.

3. Recount a time in your life when it seemed as if God wasn't around for you to find.

4. According to Hebrews 11:27, what principle did Moses practice that will help you to endure?

Now as you watch this drama unfold, remember Who wrote the script, realize Who directed the action, and recognize Who the principal actor was—God Himself. Behold the invisible yet invincible God at work, and remember that He is at work in your life as well.

The Sovereign of History

The plot of the narrative revolves around the survival of the Jewish people who stood on the threshold of a holocaust. The preservation of the nation—as well as the promise of God to bless the world and bring ultimate deliverance through the Messiah—was at stake. How would God protect His people and safeguard His promise? What means would He utilize? On this occasion He did not use the spectacular or supernatural; He used the ordinary circumstances of everyday life. This account reminds us that He is the God of not only the miraculous but also of the mundane.

5. Reflecting on Romans 11:33–36, list some of the wonderful and mysterious works and ways of God that cause you to marvel.

The account began in the city of Shushan (Susa) at the winter palace of Ahasuerus, the king of Persia. The year was 482 BC, the third year of his reign (Esther 1:3). Also known by his Greek name, Xerxes, the king was preparing to wage a military campaign against Greece, seeking revenge for a defeat his father had suffered at the hand of the Athenians at the Battle of Marathon in 490 BC. In preparation for this campaign, he called together all the nobility and leaders of his vast kingdom for a 180-day party.

6. Read Esther 1:1–4. Why did Ahasuerus gather the nobles and leaders of his vast kingdom?

7. Imagine you were part of Ahasuerus's gathering and you knew nothing of God. What might your impressions of Ahasuerus have been after taking part in his festivities?

At the end of the six-month festival, Ahasuerus held a <u>seven-day feast</u> for everyone <u>in the palace</u>, both small and great (1:5). This was probably a feast for all of those who had visited during the preceding six months. Ahasuerus brought them all together <u>to gain their support before invading Greece</u>.

8. Read Esther 1:5–8. What three words would you use to describe Ahasuerus?

9. What do you think motivated the king's generosity? Did he care about people, or did he crave <u>the praise and approval</u> of those he wined and dined?

While the king held his bash for the men in the court of the garden, Queen Vashti staged a feast for the women inside the king's house (v. 9). It was a party to end all parties, and what an ending it had!

On the last day of the feast, the inebriated king sent his seven eunuchs to summon his queen, for she was to be his late but lovely addition to the program (vv. 10, 11). "What better way," thought the king, "to conclude six months of displaying the splendor of my kingdom than to parade in front of everyone the beauty of Vashti." However, the queen was less than impressed with her partner's proposal; and being <u>concerned for her dignity</u> before that drunken crowd, she rejected the invitation.

10. Read Esther 1:12. Vashti's defiance showed that Ahasuerus couldn't control his wife, much less his empire. What did his reaction say about his ability to control himself? (See Proverbs 16:32.)

11. Ahasuerus tried to control others to please himself. What three words would you use to describe the purposes of God's providence as recorded in Romans 8:28–39?

Vashti's public snub infuriated the king and trampled his pride. So he asked his advisors how he should respond. Memucan warned the king that Vashti's action would become a standard for all the women in the kingdom if it went unchallenged (Esther 1:16–18). His only proper recourse was to act immediately by royal decree, removing Vashti permanently from her place and reaffirming the absolute authority of every man in his own house. Pleased with this counsel, Ahasuerus enacted such an edict, and the defiant Vashti was demoted (vv. 19–22).

12. What words in Esther 1:19 show God's providence and prepare the way for the entrance of Esther?

The statement that introduces the second chapter, "After these things . . . he remembered," encompasses a period of four years, from the time of Vashti's demotion in the third year of the king's reign until the promotion of Esther in the seventh year (2:16). During this gap of time Ahasuerus had been involved in waging his war with Greece. The military campaign that began in the spring of 483 BC concluded with some staggering losses in 479 BC. His vast army and navy were humiliated.

Demoralized and depressed from failing to avenge his father's defeats, the king began to recall with affection his former queen and the companionship she had provided. In an effort to bolster the king's fallen spirits, his servants proposed that a search for a new queen begin at once. But on this occasion they recommended a unique plan. Instead of selecting a queen from the small pool of nobility as was the custom, the king would choose from beautiful women from throughout the empire. The women would be taken to Shushan, the palace, and placed in the king's harem from which Ahasuerus would choose his new queen. With the king's overwhelming approval, a kingdom-wide contest was put into motion (vv. 1–4). Who would be chosen from among all the women of the kingdom? Who would win against these great odds?

The Guarantor of Victory

Humanly speaking, the odds were against Esther. The Bible identifies her as an orphaned Jewish girl, raised by her elder cousin, Mordecai. Mordecai's great-grandfather had been taken captive and deported to Babylon in 597 BC (vv. 5–7).

Though God's name is nowhere to be found in this book, His fingerprints are everywhere! The eye of faith won't miss a smudge, even on the heart of the king! Proverbs 21:1 tells us, "The king's heart is in the hand of the LORD, as the rivers of water: he turneth it whithersoever he will."

13. Read Esther 2:8–18. How do you see God's providential hand at work in bringing Esther to the throne in Persia?

14. What do you think Esther was thinking through all of this?

For the believer, the ultimate victory is certain. The final outcome is settled: the mysterious providence of God flows beneath the surface to bring deliverance to His people.

God has promised to work all things together for our good, if we are His children as evidenced by our calling and love for Him (Romans 8:28). He is conforming us to the image of His Son, Jesus Christ. Though we may not always understand or comprehend the means He uses, we know His plan for us. We can count on Him to provide for and protect us, to preserve and perfect us, just as He has promised in His Word. This God of mystery is the sovereign of history, and He has guaranteed a victory—for Israel and for us. No adversary will triumph over Him! No obstacle will block Him! He is at work in your life today. Do you have eyes to see Him and faith to trust Him?

Making It Personal

15. Place a check next to each application you would like to concentrate on this week.

❏ I will acknowledge by faith the providential working of God in my life.

❏ I will admit to God any resentment or bitterness over past life events and will renew my trust in Him for my present walk and future hope.

❏ I will aspire to trust God unconditionally in all things, demonstrating a living hope even when I may not see or understand what God is doing.

16. Memorize Romans 8:28.

The Giver of Hope

God gives hope in hopeless situations.

Esther 2:21—3:15

"Remember the word unto thy servant, upon which thou hast caused me to hope. This is my comfort in my affliction: for thy word hath quickened me" (Psalm 119:49, 50).

All people need someone or something to which they can anchor their lives—someone or something in which they can hope. A hymn asks, "Will your anchor hold in the storms of life?" The hymnwriter went on to state, "We have an anchor that keeps the soul / Steadfast and sure while the billows roll, / Fastened to the Rock which cannot move, / Grounded firm and deep in the Savior's love." These are comforting words to a believer who is facing circumstances that seem hopeless.

Mordecai and the rest of the Jews in Persia faced a seemingly hopeless situation. But they still had hope, for God was steadfast and sure.

Getting Started

1. When has hopelessness threatened to overwhelm you?

2. What did you do to overcome your hopelessness?

Searching the Scriptures

As a result of their disobedience, the people of Israel served a time of captivity. But the third chapter of Esther reveals a plan for the destruction of the nation. The promise of God to bless the world through Israel and ultimately through the Messiah was at stake. Once again the people of God became the objects of persecution and suffering.

As the second chapter of Esther closes and the third chapter opens, the storm clouds of suffering and persecution began to gather. The conflict of chapter 1 (between the king and his queen) gave way to a greater, more significant conflict in chapter 3 (between the Jews and their enemies). The conflict mounted to a crisis as the nation of Israel faced the threat of annihilation. But before the book of Esther unfolds this plot, an important parenthesis is provided at the close of the second chapter.

Providential Parenthesis

One day in the course of his official duties, Mordecai overheard two chamberlains planning to assassinate King Ahasuerus. Whatever the cause, the anger of Bigthan and Teresh boiled to the point of murder. Upon discovering their plan, Mordecai passed the information on to Queen Esther, who in turn confided the conspiracy to the king. Swift judgment followed the inquiry, and the conspirators were hanged as a warning to others.

3. Read Esther 2:21–23. How could God have used the incident to help the Jews at that point in their history?

4. What might Esther and Mordecai have thought when Mordecai received no reward or recognition from the king?

5. Describe a time when you felt God didn't take advantage of an opportunity; for example, an unbelieving friend agrees to attend a special function at his believing friend's church but cancels because of illness.

God can be trusted even when He passes on what seems to be a great opportunity to further His work. As in the case of Mordecai, sometimes a missed opportunity opens the door for a greater opportunity. The whole event—including Mordecai's discovery (see 6:2)—was permanently preserved in the official records of Persia. It was the historical record of this event that God later used as part of His plan to deliver His people. He used even the wicked intentions of those two conspirators to bring about His good pleasure. This principle is clearly seen in Proverbs 19:21—"There are many devices in a man's heart; nevertheless the counsel of the LORD, that shall stand."

Mordecai Stands Tall

Chapter 3 opens with an important promotion. After the events that had transpired, it seems Mordecai would be promoted, right? Wrong! If you have ever found yourself saying, "Life isn't fair," you can identify with Mordecai. Being bypassed for a promotion when you deserve one can be tough. But when the person promoted is your antagonist to whom you must show respect and honor, it is even more difficult. For reasons known only to King Ahasuerus, he appointed Haman prime minister of Persia. He became second to the king and, therefore, deserved the same homage. All the king's servants who sat in the gate, including Mordecai, were to bow in reverence to him.

For several days, and possibly weeks, Haman passed through the king's gate oblivious that Mordecai was not bowing with the crowd. Though other servants questioned Mordecai, they gained no response from him; but at some point in their discussions Mordecai disclosed to them his Jewish nationality. Finally, getting no cooperation from Mordecai, they informed Haman of this continual disrespect (3:4). So the next time Haman passed through the gate, he watched to see this stubborn refusal for himself. Sure enough, Mordecai stood tall and would not bow with the rest.

Filled with _rage_ that extended beyond Mordecai, Haman determined _to destroy all the Jews_ (v. 6). His vengeful response betrayed a deep-seated hatred that may have been fomenting for some time. This act of defiance combined with Haman's recent appointment to a powerful position created the perfect opportunity to vent his wrath. But behind this prejudice and planned destruction we must see the opposition of the great adversary of God's people. Unless we recognize Satan's purposes toward Israel, we cannot fully understand the tremendous struggle for the survival of God's people that this book clearly portrays. Israel is God's Chosen Nation and, therefore, Satan's choice target.

6. Read Esther 3:5 and 6. How should a believer respond to the notion that life should be fair?

We can still trust God even though we may feel as if we are being punished for doing what is right. Mordecai hoped in God and found courage in that hope.

Haman's Perilous Plot

Determined to carry out the intentions of his wicked heart, Haman sought direction from the Persian gods through the casting of lots to ascertain the best time for the massacre. The lots fell to the thirteenth day of the month of Adar, eleven months away. Though Haman trusted in chance and fate, the lots landed on the time of God's choosing. The late date of the massacre would provide time for God's planned deliverance.

7. Read Proverbs 16:33. What does this verse say about the casting of lots?

Having secured the preferred time from the astrologers and magi, Haman next sought permission from the king. Haman reported that a troublesome people were scattered throughout the empire (Esther 3:8). He claimed that they did not keep the king's laws but practiced their own instead. He then proposed his solution to this problem—destroy this rebellious element (v. 9). In return, Haman promised ten thousand talents of silver to the royal treasury. This amount was approximately 375 tons and is estimated to have been equivalent to two-thirds of the Persian empire's annual income! Obviously Haman planned to gain this amount from the expected spoils of victory. The money would appeal to Ahasuerus because his coffers had been depleted by his exploits in Greece.

8. Read Esther 3:5–9 and Proverbs 6:16–19. Which characteristics that God hates did Haman depict?

Ahasuerus's Stamp of Approval

Showing great confidence in Haman, King Ahasuerus removed his royal signet ring and gave it to Haman, who then had full authority to carry out his treacherous plot.

9. Read Esther 3:10 and 11. With the passing of Ahasuerus's signet ring to Haman, what hope, if any, was left for the Jews outside of God's divine intervention?

The official documents were drafted and sent throughout the kingdom (v. 12). The wheels had been set in motion. The annihilation of the Jewish people throughout the entire empire had been decreed.

10. Imagine you were a Jew in Persia. When the decree was read in your town square, would you have tried to escape, hide from, or fight the coming genocide?

11. What are some common ways of dealing with hopeless situations today?

The thirteenth of Adar loomed heavily over God's people. Racial hatred filled with satanic venom would soon issue in a bloodbath of destruction. As the curtain dropped on Act II, a crisis had arisen from the conflict. No single person, no clever plan, and no amount of resistance could help the Jews. Their only hope was to look to the Lord. God wanted the circumstances to be such. He allowed the events so that He might demonstrate that He is worthy of hope.

12. Read Esther 3:15. What did Haman and the king do after the death warrants had been sent throughout the kingdom?

Confusion and Hopelessness

While the king and Haman relaxed, the city of Shushan was confused. A sudden change in policy rattled not only the Jews but probably other nationalities as well. Don't overlook what God was doing here. He was shaking up the lives of the Jews, as well as every captive who had reached a level of comfort as a resident in Persia. What a great opportunity God had to show His sovereignty and power to all the captives of Persia in a time of confusion and hopelessness. (See Esther 8:17.)

13. Evaluate this statement: the more hopeless our situation, the greater the opportunity we have to shine for the Lord.

14. What can others learn about God from watching believers in hopeless situations?

15. List some Bible characters who stood for God in hopeless situations and thereby magnified God.

Making It Personal

Your ultimate hope as a believer lies in the guarantee of your salvation. No matter what happens, you can count on eternity in Heaven. You will never be utterly hopeless as a believer. Your life is firmly anchored to God, your Rock.

16. Praise God for the ultimate hope salvation gives to you.

17. Read Psalm 119:49 and 50. What are some of God's promises to you that give you hope when you face hard circumstances?

18. Create a metaphor to describe the hope God offers you. For example, *My hope in God is like an anchor secured to a rock.*

My hope in God is . . .

19. Memorize Psalm 119:49 and 50.

Lesson 11

Courage to Answer God's Call

God's people must be willing to courageously stand for Him regardless of the cost.

Esther 4:1—5:8

"Then Esther bade them return Mordecai this answer, Go, gather together all the Jews that are present in Shushan, and fast ye for me, and neither eat nor drink three days, night or day: I also and my maidens will fast likewise; and so will I go in unto the king, which is not according to the law: and if I perish, I perish" (Esther 4:15, 16).

During the student revolution that took place in China in the spring and summer of 1989, a young man demonstrated what courage is all about. Numerous news agencies carried the footage of an amazing scene that took place in Tiananmen Square in Beijing. One young man, alone and unidentified, stood in the path of a convoy of tanks. As the lead tank attempted to maneuver around him, the man moved to prevent it. He simply refused to bow to the military might that confronted him. He did not run in fear. He did not stay where he was comfortable. He courageously stood his ground on the front lines.

God has called us as believers to stand for Christ and to represent

Him to our generation. Yet few of us stand for Christ as we should. We are immobilized by fear instead of energized by faith. How we need the courage of an Esther who said, "If I perish, I perish." We must recognize the divine appointment of God's providence and serve Him in our generation.

Getting Started

1. Can every believer be courageous? Explain.

2. Do you consider yourself a courageous believer? Why or why not?

Searching the Scriptures

Agonizing before God

As the fourth chapter of Esther opens, we discover that the conflict that started between Haman and Mordecai had indeed escalated and reached the point of crisis for the Jews. The curtain is lifted, and we see Mordecai in agony (Esther 4:1).

3. Read Esther 4:1 and 2. What did Mordecai do when he learned of Haman's plot?

4. How much courage did it take for Mordecai to openly display his Jewish heritage to the whole city?

5. What did Mordecai demonstrate to God by his actions?

As word of Haman's destructive plan swept the empire, the lamentation of God's Chosen People could be heard in every province (v. 3).

Esther learned of Mordecai's actions and sent new clothes to replace his sackcloth. She was concerned that the king might make an appearance and be offended by Mordecai's sackcloth. But Mordecai refused to receive it. Confused and concerned with this response, Esther sent a trusted chamberlain to discover the reason for her cousin's great sorrow. Mordecai related the dire news to Esther, providing her with a copy of the edict that called for the destruction of the Jews. With this distressing information, Mordecai also sent disturbing instructions to Esther: go to the king and intercede on behalf of your people (vv. 5–9).

6. Read Esther 4:10–12. What two words would you use to describe Esther's response to Mordecai's plea?

Esther had no way of knowing how Ahasuerus might respond to an unsolicited visit. She could possibly forfeit her life for such a brazen act. At least initially, that was a chance she was unwilling to take.

Mordecai's reply to Esther's fear is the pivotal text and central message of the account.

7. Read Esther 4:13 and 14. Summarize Mordecai's response to Esther.

Deliverance Will Arise

If Esther decided not to take action, deliverance would still arise, but from another place. That is the message of the book of Esther: deliverance will arise. You can depend on it. God has promised to preserve and protect His people. His providence will not allow His promise to fail.

8. Have you ever wondered how God was going to work together all things for good in your life? In 2 Corinthians 1:8–11 Paul recalled how God had delivered him. What lessons did Paul learn through God's deliverance?

The question was not, Would God deliver His people? but rather, How would God deliver His people? Mordecai had realized that the providence of God had brought Esther to that crucial point. She would need courage to face the conflict and to speak on behalf of her people.

9. Review the familiar account of the fiery furnace in Daniel 3. According to their words in verses 17 and 18, what did Daniel's companions believe about their God?

10. What were they willing to do to demonstrate their commitment to Him?

Those three men understood that God's reputation was on the line. Their commitment to His will would not allow them to go with the crowd. Dynamic faith overcame debilitating fear, and they stood for God against the world. Consequently, God stood with them. (See 2 Timothy 4:16–18.)

Standing alone and sacrificing all is a high price tag for representing God. But Someone stood alone and sacrificed everything for us. Jesus Christ was truly alone, as both God and people forsook him (Matthew 26:31; 27:46). He made the greatest sacrifice, shedding His blood for us, taking our sin so we might receive His righteousness (1 Peter 2:24; 2 Corinthians 5:21). But when we take a stand for God, we are never really alone, for God stands with us. Our sacrifice will never match His. And if in God's providence we are called to lay down our lives, Paul would remind us in Philippians 1:21 that even this "sacrifice" is gain!

11. What does God call believers to do that requires courage?

Love for Comfort and Fear of Loss

Why do we find it difficult to stand for Christ? Why don't we follow in His steps as we know we should? Why do we struggle with total commitment? It is because we face the same barriers that Esther faced, a love for comfort and a fear of loss. They go hand in hand.

Consider Esther's situation. She was the queen of the Persian Empire. For five years Esther had enjoyed all the luxuries of her culture. Servants waited on her every need. The finest in fashion and the most exquisite cuisine were at her disposal. She resided in a magnificent palace. All the women in the empire envied her. Not bad for an orphan immigrant! Why should she rock the boat when things were going so well? No one else knew she was a Jew. She had been going undercover, comfortable in that pagan culture. Why expose herself? Why jeopardize her position? It would take tremendous courage to sacrifice the comfort she enjoyed and stand with the people of God.

12. Read Esther 4:15 and 16. What decision did Esther make?

13. What did Esther communicate to God by taking three days for fasting?

Esther sent word to Mordecai to notify him of her decision and to request his help. He was to gather all the Jews in Shushan and fast for three days. Though the account does not mention prayer, it does imply that the Jews prayed. Esther needed courage to follow through on her decision, and she wanted all the support possible (vv. 15, 16).

Like Esther, we must be willing to dash our desire for comfort on the rock of obedience. We must count it greater gain to lose our lives for Christ. We must determine that the greater honor is ours when the world considers us fools for Christ and condemns us rather than commends us. If we are going to be faithful to our calling and represent God to our generation, we must have courage to go against the current of our culture, facing the conflict and following Christ.

Prayer and Fasting

Three days of prayer and fasting could either make or break Esther's commitment. Imagine the pressure and fear she experienced! Maybe she thought of all the "what ifs": "What if the king will not receive me? What if he moves up the date of the destruction out of anger? What if he has me executed? What if I don't follow through with this plan? What if I just wait it out?"

14. What fears often keep believers from standing for God and obeying Him?

Have you ever allowed fear to hinder you from following through on a decision to stand or speak for Christ? You wouldn't be the first. According to John 20:19, Jesus found His followers—the ones who had just four days earlier said they would never deny Him—behind closed doors "for fear of the Jews." Ten out of twelve spies persuaded the Children of Israel not to enter the Promised Land because they feared the inhabitants (Numbers 13:31–33). The Israelites ran for cover in the Valley of Elah out of fear of Goliath (1 Samuel 17:24).

15. What does Proverbs 29:25 exhort us to do in place of fearing people?

16. What promises in Deuteronomy 31:6 will help us gain the courage we need to stand for Christ?

Whether Esther consciously knew it or not, God was there that day as she entered the inner court of Ahasuerus. Dressed in her royal apparel, she stepped into the presence of the king, unaware that the King of Kings, Who rules the affairs of mankind, was providentially protecting her. He was working all things together for her good and for His glory. He Who can turn the king's heart like the rivers of water had prepared this monarch. Esther had fixed her eyes on the golden scepter in the king's hand. The moment of truth had come, and her courage was rewarded as the king extended the scepter to her. What suspense! What relief! What rejoicing! Her reception was more than she could have imagined as the king offered to answer her request up to half of the kingdom (Esther 5:1–3).

17. How does a believer feel after courageously obeying God? Can any comfort or amount of safety compare to the satisfaction of standing up for God? (See the example of Paul and Silas in Acts 16:22–25.)

Confronting Fear

Again we see the overruling providence of God as Esther waited for the best time to make her request of the king. It would come at a second banquet to which she would invite the king and Haman. We do not know why she did not make her request at the first banquet. She may have determined that gaining the king's acceptance was accomplishment enough for one day and that she shouldn't press too hard. But whatever her reasoning, the divine purpose was being accomplished. God had two more important events to unfold before Esther would make known her concern.

Esther had done her part. She had confronted her fear, abandoned her comfort zone, and courageously risked her life for the sake of her people. Her decision to reveal her nationality showed her loyalty to God.

God wants us, like Esther, to overcome any lack of courage and love of comfort. He wants us to courageously stand for Him regardless of the cost.

Making It Personal

18. What is God calling you to do that you don't feel courageous enough to do?

19. Express to God your decision to trust Him for courage to do what He wants you to do. Consider following Esther's example and taking extra time to pray about your fears.

20. What one courageous act can you do for the Lord this week?

21. Memorize Esther 4:15 and 16 as a reminder of Esther's courageous stand for God.

The Perils of Pride

Pride is destructive.

Esther 5:9—7:10

"But he giveth more grace. Wherefore he saith, God resisteth the proud, but giveth grace unto the humble" (James 4:6).

Accompanied by two stalwart guides, a young stranger to the Alps made his first climb up the mountains. The ascent was steep and hazardous. For hours they climbed the rugged and treacherous slope together. Although breathless, they finally reached the rocks protruding through the snow above them—the summit. They had made it! Only the final task of topping the peak remained. Forgetting the strong gales that blow across the summit, the eager young man leaped to his feet. But as he did, the chief guide quickly grabbed him and dragged him down. "On your knees, sir!" he shouted. "You are never safe here except on your knees."

The young climber would risk a great fall if he were to stand on that summit. His guide was right, for he had been there before and knew the potential danger. The only safe position in that place was on one's knees, demonstrating a proper reverence and fear for the elements.

That is a great picture of our relationship with and approach to God. We must come "on our knees" with a proper sense of reverence and fear, recognizing Who He is and who we are in relation to Him.

He is the holy creator; we are His fallen creatures. There is no place for pride. There is no room for standing defiantly in His presence. To do so is to risk a great fall (Proverbs 16:18).

Getting Started

1. Why is pride such an affront to God?

2. Why does pride inevitably lead to a fall?

Searching the Scriptures

Completely purifying our motives of sinful pride is an ongoing and difficult battle. But it is a battle that we must wage so we can walk with Christ and follow in His steps. He calls us to take up His yoke and learn of Him, for He is meek and lowly (Matthew 11:29). So as we examine the pride of mankind and its resulting consequences, let us remember that we are not immune to pride's sway.

3. How does Psalm 10:4 describe a proud person?

4. What place does God have in a proud person's life?

Haman's Pride

The focus of the narrative shifts to Haman in Esther 5:9. The first of two private banquets hosted by the queen had just concluded (vv. 5–8). Other than King Ahasuerus, Haman was the only individual invited. As

he returned home from this first banquet, he was filled with pride. His
self-esteem couldn't have been any higher. All was right in Haman's
world. He was second only to the king. The destruction of the Jewish
people was a done deal. And now he was dining with the king and
queen! He was at the pinnacle of his career. He hurried home to boast
to his wife and his friends about the honor that had been granted to
him alone.

Yes, all was right in Haman's world—except for one small matter.
As he journeyed home to break the good news, he passed through the
king's gate. And there, standing out like a scarecrow in a cornfield
after harvest, was that unbending, non-bowing, unbearable Jew named
Mordecai. Haman just couldn't handle seeing him every time he passed
through the gate. And though that evening he enjoyed bragging of his
riches, his privileged position, and the stature of his family in the kingdom, those things didn't please him as long as Mordecai still stood before his eyes (vv. 9–13). Like a deep scratch on a new car, the continual
presence of Mordecai ruined the finish on Haman's joy. He just couldn't
forget about that bothersome Mordecai.

5. Read Esther 5:9–13. How would you describe Haman based on
these verses?

6. What historical figures remind you of Haman?

7. What response would you have given Haman if you had been
with him to hear his bragging and his anger over Mordecai?

Haman's Murderous Plot

Concerned only for his happiness, Haman's friends and family encouraged Haman to use his newfound power to put away Mordecai for

good. They counseled him to use his clout and have a seventy-five-foot gallows erected that night. You can just about hear his wife, Zeresh, say to him in effect, "Build it tonight. Hang Mordecai in the morning. Enjoy your banquet in the evening. No problem." Pleased with the advice of his wife and friends, Haman immediately enlisted a governmental crew to complete the project by morning (5:14).

As the sun went down that evening, the action reached its climax. Against a darkening sky the gallows rose high. And in the quiet evening hours designed for rest, hammers pounded. The nation of Israel had already been fitted for destruction, and Mordecai would be the first to fall. Esther would be left alone to face the devices of Haman, who had the king's full confidence and cooperation. As chapter 5 closes, it appears that all was lost.

The beauty of this account—and of all history—lies in the fact that a divine but often hidden perspective exists. When the sun finally set below the horizon and the gallows stood finished above it, God began to reveal what had always been true: although all seems lost, it isn't. When God seems absent, He isn't. God is in control. He has been there all along. Though we may not understand all the details of the plan, we can trust His promise. In working out this situation, God accomplished two things: "save the afflicted people" and "bring down high looks" (Psalm 18:27). God is indeed able to turn apparent tragedy into amazing triumph. And He did for Mordecai, Esther, and the Jews.

8. List other Biblical examples in which God turned apparent tragedy into triumph.

Haman's Surprise

Of all nights, on that particular night the king could not sleep. Maybe he was puzzled over Esther's upcoming request. Maybe he had eaten something that didn't agree with him. Regardless of what caused the king's sleeplessness, we know that his insomnia was divinely appointed. The king needed to know something, so he was awakened by the providence of God. He called for the royal chronicles to be read—a logical choice to cure insomnia!

9. Read Esther 6:1–3. What did the king discover from the chronicles?

Apparently the king listened to the records being read throughout the entire night. The king inquired concerning who was standing in the court (6:4). And there was Haman, ready to begin the business day early. He was eager to carry out his mission and gain permission to execute Mordecai on the newly constructed gallows.

10. Read Esther 6:4 and 5. What is your reaction when you reach this point in the account? Can you read these verses without at least cracking a smile?

The king had Haman brought in and posed a question to him: "What shall be done unto the man whom the king delighteth to honour?" Thinking that the king was, of course, referring to him (for that is all a proud heart thinks about—himself), Haman quickly proposed that he be treated as royalty and be led through the streets by a noble who would proclaim his honor.

Haman's hope was high and his expectation certain. He watched the king's expression and saw his positive response. Certainly Haman was imagining the weight of the royal robe around his shoulders at that moment. He could feel the powerful steed beneath him and hear the applause of people around him. How could it be otherwise? Who else would the king wish to honor?

11. On the empty face below, draw an expression that reflects what Haman might have looked like as he left to carry out the king's instructions (v. 10). Horror-stricken by the king's command, Haman could do nothing but obey.

Following this public and profound humiliation, Haman returned home with his head covered as a sign of grief. His counselors, who just the day before had helped plan his victory, had a different message for Haman.

12. Read Esther 6:13. Why do you suppose Haman's wife and advisors changed their message to Haman?

Before Haman could draw up contingency plans, the king's eunuchs arrived to take him to the banquet Esther had prepared.

Haman's Demise

At the banquet Esther finally made her petition known to the king. She entreated Ahasuerus to save her and her people from impending destruction. Her revelation truly surprised him, for the king had been unaware that his queen was Jewish. Apparently this fact was news to Haman as well. The angered king immediately demanded the identity of the enemy. Haman's day had just gone from bad to worse. The queen turned and pointed her finger at Haman and said, "The adversary and enemy is this wicked Haman" (Esther 7:6).

13. On the empty face below, draw an expression that reflects
what Haman might have looked like as he heard the queen's words in
Esther 7:6.

Filled with rage, the king left the banquet room and headed into
the adjoining garden to decide his course of action. Haman, fully aware
that his life was hanging in the balance, threw himself on the queen's
couch to beg for mercy (v. 7). But at that moment the king returned and
mistook Haman's actions as a violent attack upon his queen (v. 8).

14. What thought must have gone through Haman's mind immediately after being accused of attacking Esther?

The king ordered the executioners to take Haman away. As they did
so, one of the courtiers informed the king that the newly erected gallows—which would have been visible from the palace—had been built
by Haman and designed for Mordecai. With a stroke of poetic justice,
the king put them to good use and had Haman hanged (vv. 9, 10).

A southern expression fits Haman's experience: Why am I always
getting my britches stuck on my own pitchfork?

15. Read Psalm 9:15 and 16. What truths in these verses are reflective
of Haman's life?

Haman had indeed been caught in his own net. Pride had domi-
nated his life and ultimately destroyed him. His fall was rapid and
revealing. It revealed the destructive character and the dangerous consequences of pride. As Proverbs 15:25 states, "The LORD will destroy the
house of the proud." God is able to abase those who walk in pride.

16. Since pride is such a dangerous and destructive condition of
the heart, how can we avoid it? Read 1 Corinthians 1:26–31 and James
4:6–10 and record the truths from these passages.

One of the sidelights of this part of the narrative is the principle of
waiting on God for exaltation and vindication. Esther 2 records Mordecai's discovery of the assassination plot against the king. Mordecai went
unrewarded. He was passed over, and the promotion went to Haman.
Life certainly didn't appear to be fair at that point! But in due time—
God's time—the reward came. It came at the right time. God's promotions, if we are willing to wait for them, will always be the best.

Making It Personal

17. How entrenched is pride in your life? Check all the following de-
scriptions that apply to you, or add your own observations about yourself.

❑ I talk about myself a lot (Esther 5:11, 12).

❑ I can't stand anyone who doesn't gush over me (5:9, 13).

❑ I count on myself to solve my problems.

❑ I rejoice in the downfall of others (5:14).

❏ I think of myself as better than anyone else (6:6).

❏ I don't like to see others succeed (6:12).

❏ I don't admit when I am wrong (7:7).

18. What destruction might come your way if you don't deal with any pride in your life right now (Proverbs 16:18)?

19. What action do you need to take in dealing with any pride in your life? (See question 16.)

20. Memorize James 4:6.

Celebrating God

God is worthy of celebration.

Esther 8—10

"Let all those that seek thee rejoice and be glad in thee: let such as love thy salvation say continually, The LORD be magnified" (Psalm 40:16).

The last Sunday in August is the day the Philippines sets aside for National Heroes' Day. In 2004 that holiday fell on the 31st. On that same day, Kyrgyzstan, Trinidad, and Tobago each celebrate their Independence Day. Malaysia recognizes August 31 as its National Day, while Moldova uses that day for National Language Day. Australia's White Rose Day (in honor of Princess Diana) also falls on August 31.

Choose any other day of the year and you will find at least one country celebrating a holiday. Every day is a holiday somewhere in the world. If you had the time and the money, you could travel around the world and join a different celebration each day. Or you could stay home and tell your boss that you won't be at work because it's September 1 and you are recognizing Slovakia's Constitution Day. The next day you could tell your boss you will be absent because you want to celebrate Vietnam's National Day. Of course by the next day you won't have to call your boss, since most likely you won't have a job anymore.

Esther and Mordecai set up a holiday that is now celebrated in March. Called the Feast of Purim, the holiday commemorates the Jews' deliverance from their enemies. The Feast of Purim and the events that led up to its establishment are the focus of the last three chapters of Esther. As you study how the holiday came about, you will be challenged to celebrate God every day of your life.

Getting Started

1. What is the most memorable celebration you have ever attended?

2. What do you think a celebration for God should include?

Searching the Scriptures

Chapter 8 of Esther opens with Ahasuerus giving Haman's wealth to Esther.

3. Read Esther 8:1. What would you expect someone to do after receiving an immense amount of wealth?

Esther revealed to the king her family relationship to Mordecai; and in the wake of the overthrow of Haman, the king granted Mordecai Haman's position. He received the royal signet ring as a symbol of that transfer of authority. Esther then appointed Mordecai as the manager of Haman's great riches. But all was not well (Esther 8:2).

Asking for Mercy

The king's edict calling for the destruction of the Jews was still in force, and the thirteenth of Adar loomed ominous before them. So Esther once again risked her life by going in before the king unannounced to beg for the life of her people. Forgetting her newfound wealth, Esther poured out her heart for her people before the king. Again the king graciously accepted her (vv. 3, 4).

4. Read Esther 8:3–6. Describe Esther's concern for her people.

5. Compare what Esther said she couldn't live without (Esther 8:6) with what Haman had said he couldn't live without (5:13).

Due to the nature of Persian law, the king's hands were tied. Ahasuerus was unable to repeal the law, although he wished he could.

A New Decree

In seeking a remedy to the dilemma, the king pointed out some important facts and then ordered Mordecai and Esther to draft a decree of their own (8:7, 8).

6. Read Esther 8:7. What two facts did the king point out to Mordecai and Esther?

7. Why might these truths have helped them in their endeavor to save Israel?

Ahasuerus instructed Esther and Mordecai to seal their decree with his signet ring to make it as binding as the decree that Haman had written. Mordecai then gathered the king's scribes and had the decree written in all the languages of the people of Persia.

8. Read Esther 8:11. Does the summary of the declaration surprise you? Did you expect it to say something else? If so, what?

At least 127 copies of the decree were made and sent into all the provinces of Persia. Men on swift horses pressed on by order of the king until each province heard the declaration.

9. Read Esther 8:15–17. How did the Jews respond to the declaration?

Also as a result of the declaration, many Gentiles became Jews, not in the full sense of a proselyte; but rather, they identified themselves with the Jewish people for fear of being wrongly identified as enemies (v. 17).

Most certainly Mordecai included in his declaration the account of Haman's failed attempt to kill the Jews. In essence, Haman was set up as an example of what would happen to all those who tried to lift a finger against the Jews. In this way Haman's actions sealed the fate of his family and the enemies of the Jews. His example showed the entire empire that there was no way the Jews' enemies could win. In addition, Haman's former wealth, now in the hands of Esther and Mordecai, could have easily funded the buying and making of swords and other weapons for the Jews to use in defending themselves. No wonder the Jews were celebrating even though the decree to annihilate their people was still a valid law.

10. Who were the Jews ultimately celebrating?

The Day of Deliverance

When the thirteenth of Adar (March 7, 473 BC) arrived, and the two contradictory decrees took effect, the Jews of Persia fought valiantly for their lives (9:2).

11. Read Esther 9:1–5. What evidence do you see that the victories the Jews enjoyed weren't simply a result of their valiant efforts?

When the fighting was over, the enemies of God's people had been killed—seventy-five thousand in the provinces, eight hundred in the capital of Shushan, and the ten sons of Haman, who had been hanged on the gallows to prevent family reprisals (vv. 6–15).

12. The end of verses 10, 15, and 16 of chapter 9 stress that the Jews did not take any spoils from their victory. Why did this point receive such emphasis?

With the one-day war in the provinces and the two-day war in the capital of Shushan finished, it was time to feast (v. 17).

Days of Remembrance

To remember God's mighty deliverance, Mordecai sent word throughout the empire that two days, the fourteenth and fifteenth of Adar, be kept annually as days of remembrance.

13. Read Esther 9:19–25. Why would the Jews include giving gifts in their feast?

14. Read Esther 9:26. How does the name of the feast, Purim, help Jews remember to celebrate the providence of God? (See Esther 3:7.)

15. What commitments did the Jews make surrounding the Feast of Purim (9:27, 28)?

16. What effects might these annual celebrations of God have had on their children and future generations?

Since Israel's day of deliverance, the nation has celebrated Purim with feasting and joy, the sharing of goods, and the giving of gifts. The principal ceremony of Purim involves the reading of the book of Esther in the synagogue. When Haman's name is read from the scroll of Esther, it is met by a thunderous roar of clapping hands, stomping feet, booing, hissing, and, at times, the grinding noise of groggers (handheld noise-makers made especially for drowning out Haman's name).

Primary to the Feast of Purim is the theme of celebration, a time of eating and rejoicing. The rabbis of the Talmud taught that a person should get so caught up in the joy of Purim that he or she is unable to tell the difference between "cursed be Haman" and "blessed be Morde-cai." The Jews often celebrate this holiday with costumes and carnivals.

With Purim instituted and, more importantly, Israel's enemies de-feated, all seemed at peace in the Persian kingdom. Ahasuerus sat on the throne, and Queen Esther and Mordecai, the new prime minister, ruled with him. God had indeed humbled the proud and exalted the humble. He had delivered His people as He had promised. In doing so, God spared the line of David from which Jesus was born. All believers, in that light, should rejoice in what God did in the days of Esther. By delivering the Jews, God preserved the deliverance of the world from sin through His Son, Jesus.

Even now our lives are in God's hands, and we can trust Him. He is truly worthy of celebration for what He has done for us and what He has promised yet to do.

17. How has your perspective of God's providence changed or been enhanced as a result of studying the books of Ezra and Esther?

Making It Personal

18. What has God done in your life that is worth celebrating?

19. What dates can you set aside to celebrate what God has done for you in the past? For example, choose the dates you were saved and baptized.

20. What can you do to celebrate God, even in a small way, every day of your life?

21. Memorize Psalm 40:16 and never forget to celebrate God's providence. You're in His hands, and there is no better place to be.